Lower Midwest Community Tree Guide: Benefits, Costs, and Strategic Planting

Paula J. Peper, E. Gregory McPherson, James R. Simpson, Kelaine E. Vargas, and Qingfu Xiao

U.S. Department of Agriculture, Forest Service
Pacific Southwest Research Station
Albany, California
General Technical Report PSW-GTR-219
March 2009

This work was sponsored by the U.S. Department of Agriculture, Forest Service, State and Private Forestry, Urban and Community Forestry Program; the State of Indiana Department of Natural Resources, Division of Forestry, Urban Forestry Program; and the City of Indianapolis, Department of Parks and Recreation.

Abstract

Peper, Paula J.; McPherson, E. Gregory; Simpson, James R.; Vargas, Kelaine E.; Xiao, Qingfu. 2009. Lower Midwest community tree guide: benefits, costs, and strategic planting. Gen. Tech. Rep. PSW-GTR-219. Albany, CA: U.S. Department of Agriculture, Forest Service, Pacific Southwest Research Station. 115 p.

Even as they increase the beauty of our surroundings, trees provide us with a great many ecosystem services, including air quality improvement, energy conservation, stormwater interception, and atmospheric carbon dioxide reduction. These benefits must be weighed against the costs of maintaining trees, including planting, pruning, irrigation, administration, pest control, liability, cleanup, and removal. We present benefits and costs for representative small, medium, and large deciduous trees in the Lower Midwest region derived from models based on indepth research carried out in Indianapolis, Indiana. Average annual net benefits increase with tree size and differ based on location: $4 (public) to $12 (yard) for a small tree, $12 (public) to $24 (yard) for a medium tree, and $47 (public) to $60 (yard) for a large tree. Two hypothetical examples of planting projects are described to illustrate how the data in this guide can be adapted to local uses, and guidelines for maximizing benefits and reducing costs are given.

Keywords: Ecosystem services, Lower Midwest, urban forestry, benefit-cost analysis.

In the Lower Midwest region, trees play an environmental, cultural, and historical role in communities.

Benefits and costs quantified

Summary

This report quantifies benefits and costs for representative small, medium, and large deciduous trees in the Lower Midwest region. The species chosen as representative are eastern redbud, littleleaf linden, and northern hackberry (see "Common and Scientific Names" section). The analysis describes "yard trees" (those planted in residential sites) and "public trees" (those planted on streets or in parks). Benefits are calculated based on tree growth curves and numerical models that consider regional climate, building characteristics, air pollutant concentrations, and prices. Tree care costs and mortality rates are based on results from a survey of municipal and commercial arborists. We assume a 50-percent survival rate over a 40-year timeframe.

The measurements used in modeling environmental and other benefits of trees are based on indepth research carried out in Indianapolis, Indiana. Given the Lower Midwest region's diverse geographical area, this approach provides general approximations based on some necessary assumptions that serve as a starting point for more specific local calculations. It is a general accounting that can be easily adapted and adjusted for local planting projects. Two examples are provided that illustrate how to adjust benefits and costs to reflect different aspects of local urban forest improvement projects.

Average annual benefits

Large trees provide the most benefits. Average annual benefits increase with mature tree size and differ based on tree location. The lowest values are for yard trees on the southern side of houses, and the highest values are for yard trees on the western side of houses. Values for public trees are intermediate. Average annual benefits range as follows:

- $15 to $21 for a small tree
- $27 to $35 for a medium tree
- $58 to $73 for a large tree

Benefits associated with reduced level of stormwater runoff and increased aesthetic and other benefits reflected in higher property values account for the largest proportion of total benefits in this region. Reduced levels of energy use, air pollutants, and carbon dioxide (CO_2) in the air are the next most important benefits.

Energy conservation benefits differ with tree location as well as size. Trees located opposite west-facing walls provide the greatest net heating and cooling energy savings. Reducing heating and cooling energy needs reduces CO_2 emissions and thereby reduces atmospheric CO_2. Similarly, energy savings that reduce demand from powerplants account for important reductions in gases that produce ozone, a major component of smog, and other air pollutants.

The benefits of trees are offset by the costs of caring for them. Based on our surveys of municipal and residential arborists, the average annual cost for tree care ranges from $9 to $24 per tree. (Values below are for yard and public trees, respectively.)

Costs

- $9 and $16 for a small tree
- $10 and $18 for a medium tree
- $13 and $24 for a large tree

Pruning costs, annualized over 40 years, are a significant expense ($2 to $8 per tree per year). Public trees also incur a significant administrative expense ($4 to $6 per tree per year). Planting ($4 per tree per year) and removal and disposal annualized over 40 years ($2 to $3 per tree per year) are the next greatest costs. During the establishment period, costs for labor-intensive hand watering were low, estimated to be $0.23 per year for 5 years.

Average annual net benefits

Average annual net benefits (benefits minus costs) per tree for a 40-year period differ with tree location and tree size and range from a low of $4 to a high of $60 per tree.

- $4 for a small public tree to $12 for a small yard tree on the west side of a house
- $12 for a medium public tree to $24 for a medium yard tree on the west side of a house
- $47 for a large public tree to $60 for a large yard tree on the west side of a house

Environmental benefits alone, including energy savings, stormwater runoff reduction, improved air quality, and reduced atmospheric CO_2, can be nearly twice the cost of tree care.

Net benefits summed over 40 years

Net benefits for a yard tree opposite a west wall and a public tree are substantial when summed over the 40-year period (values below are for public trees and yard trees opposite a west wall, respectively):

- $149 and $475 for a small tree
- $454 and $923 for a medium tree
- $1,809 and $2,356 for a large tree

Yard trees produce higher net benefits than public trees, primarily because of lower maintenance costs.

To demonstrate ways that communities can adapt the information in this report to their needs, examples of two fictional cities interested in improving their urban forest have been created. The benefits and costs of different planting projects are determined. In the hypothetical city of Flint Falls, net benefits and benefit-cost ratios (BCRs; total benefits divided by costs) are calculated for a planting of 1,000 trees (3-in caliper) assuming a cost of $200 per tree, 43 percent mortality rate, and 40-year analysis. Total benefits are $2.46 million, total costs are about $822,000, and net benefits are $1.63 million ($40.89 per tree per year). The BCR is 2.99:1, indicating that $2.99 is returned for every $1 invested. The net benefits and BCRs (in parentheses) by mature tree size are:

- $9,306 (1.30:1) for 50 eastern redbud trees
- $119,526 (1.80:1) for 200 littleleaf linden
- $1,506,670 (3.35:1) for 750 northern hackberry

Reduced stormwater runoff benefits account for 41 percent of the estimated benefits. Increased property values reflecting aesthetic and other benefits of trees account for 35 percent of the estimated benefits, and reduced energy costs for another 16 percent. Air quality improvement (6 percent) and atmospheric CO_2 reduction (2 percent) make up the remaining benefits.

In the fictional city of Sandy Creek, long-term planting and tree care costs and benefits were compared to determine if current fashion for planting small flowering trees instead of the large stately trees that were once standard is substantially affecting the level of benefits residents are receiving. Over a 40-year period, the net benefits are:

- $58 for a small tree
- $367 for a medium tree
- $1,668 for a large tree

Based on this analysis, the city of Sandy Creek decided to strengthen its tree ordinance, requiring developers to plant large trees wherever feasible and to create tree shade plans that show how they will achieve 50-percent shade over streets, sidewalks, and parking lots within 15 years of development.

Contents

The green infrastructure is a significant component of communities in the Lower Midwest region.

Chapter 1. Introduction

The Lower Midwest Region

From the Ouachita Mountains of Kansas and Arkansas to the bluegrass country of Kentucky, the Lower Midwest region sweeps across eight states containing a diverse assemblage of municipalities (fig. 1). The **climate**[1] of this region corresponds to Sunset climate zone 35 (Brenzel 2001) and is characterized by hot, humid summers, and winters that are cold but milder than the areas to the north. Average summer high temperatures can range from the low 100s to as high as 114 degrees Fahrenheit (F). Every few years, arctic air masses come through during winter, dropping temperatures to as low as the -20s F in northern and central portions of the region. Precipitation comes in all seasons and averages range from 36 to 42 in annually. This varies extensively with as little as 11 in falling in southeast Kansas

Scope of the Lower Midwest region

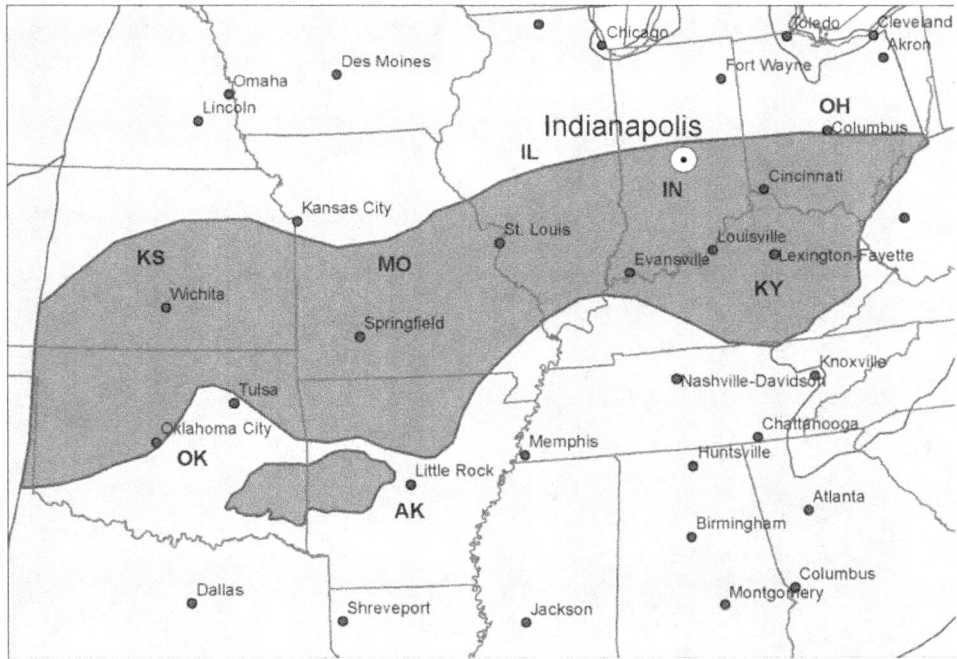

Figure 1—The Lower Midwest contains a diverse assemblage of municipalities extending from the Ouachita Mountains of Arkansas and Oklahoma to the bluegrass country of Kentucky.

---

[1] Words in bold are defined in the glossary.

Lower Midwest communities can derive many benefits from community forests

compared to over 50 in falling in Arkansas lowlands. In some areas like southern Indiana and Illinois, more rain tends to fall during warmer months when leaves are on trees than during dormant months. The growing season ranges from 150 to 240 days.

As the communities of the Lower Midwest continue to grow and change during the coming decades, growing and sustaining healthy **community forests** is integral to the quality of life that residents experience. In the Lower Midwest, the urban forest is a distinctive feature of the landscape that protects us from the elements, cleans the water we drink and the air we breathe, and forms a living connection to earlier generations who planted and tended the trees.

The role of our urban forests in enhancing the environment, increasing community attractiveness and livability, and fostering civic pride takes on greater significance as communities strive to balance economic growth with environmental quality and social well-being. Planting trees provides opportunities to connect residents with nature and with each other (fig. 2). Neighborhood tree plantings and stewardship projects stimulate investment by local citizens, businesses, and governments for the betterment of their communities. Community forests bring opportunity for economic renewal, combating development woes, improving human health, and increasing the quality of life for community residents.

Pam Louks

Figure 2—Tree planting and stewardship programs provide opportunities for local residents to work together to build better communities.

Lower Midwest communities can promote energy efficiency through tree planting and stewardship programs that strategically locate trees to save energy and minimize conflicts with urban infrastructure. The same trees can provide additional benefits by reducing stormwater runoff; improving local air, soil, and water quality; reducing atmospheric carbon dioxide (CO_2); providing wildlife habitat; increasing property values; slowing traffic; enhancing community attractiveness and investment; and promoting human well-being.

Quality of life improves with trees

Although trees can provide many benefits to residents of the Lower Midwest, there may be concern over the introduction of nonnative trees that they may prove to be invasive, particularly in riparian areas, provide habitat for nonnative fauna, and encroach on nearby native habitats. These concerns are valid, considering for example, the invasion of the tree of heaven (see "Common and Scientific Names" section) throughout the region (Midwest Invasive Plants Network 2006) and of Russian olive throughout the Western United States (Brock 1998). Careful species selection in collaboration with your local extension agent or city forester can allay these concerns while allowing local communities to reap the many benefits of trees in urban areas. It is important to maintain species and age diversity to insure the health and sustainability of the urban forest.

This guide builds upon studies by the USDA Forest Service in Chicago and Sacramento (McPherson et al. 1994, 1997), and other regional tree guides from the Center for Urban Forest Research (McPherson et al. 1999b, 2000, 2003, 2004, 2006a, 2006b, 2007; Vargas et al. 2007a, 2007b) to extend knowledge of urban forest benefits in the Lower Midwest. The guide:

Scope defined

- Quantifies benefits of trees on a per-tree basis rather than on a canopy-cover basis (it should not be used to estimate benefits for trees growing in forest stands).
- Describes management costs and benefits.
- Details how tree planting programs can improve environmental quality, conserve energy, and add value to communities.
- Explains where to place residential yard and public trees to maximize their benefits and cost-effectiveness.
- Describes ways to minimize conflicts between trees and power lines, sidewalks, and buildings.
- Illustrates how to use this information to estimate benefits and costs for local tree planting projects.

Audience and objectives

These guidelines are specific to the Lower Midwest, and are based on data and calculations from open-growing urban street trees in Indianapolis, Indiana.

Street, park, and shade trees are components of all Lower Midwest communities, and they affect every resident. Their benefits are myriad. However, with municipal tree programs dependent on taxpayer-supported general funds, communities are forced to ask whether trees are worth the price to plant and care for over the long term, thus requiring urban forestry programs to demonstrate their cost-effectiveness (McPherson 1995). If tree plantings are proven to benefit communities, then financial commitment to tree programs will be justified. Therefore, the objective of this tree guide is to identify and describe the benefits and costs of planting trees in Lower Midwest communities—providing a tool for municipal tree managers, arborists, and tree enthusiasts to increase public awareness and support for trees (Dwyer and Miller 1999).

Chapter 2. Benefits and Costs of Urban and Community Forests

This chapter describes benefits and costs of publicly and privately managed trees and presents the functional benefits and associated economic value of community forests. Expenditures related to tree care and management are assessed—a necessary process for creating cost-effective programs (Dwyer et al. 1992, Hudson 1983).

Benefits

Saving Energy

Energy is essential for quality of life and for economic growth. Conserving energy by greening our cities is often more cost-effective than building new powerplants. For example, while California was experiencing energy shortages in 2001, its 177 million city trees were providing shade and conserving energy. Annual savings to utilities were an estimated $500 million in wholesale electricity and generation purchases (McPherson and Simpson 2003). Planting 50 million more shade trees in strategic locations would provide savings equivalent to seven 100-megawatt power-plants. In 2001, it cost $150 to 250 to produce, purchase, or conserve a kW at the summertime peak. Hence, peak load reduction measures that cost less than $150 per kW saved are considered cost-effective. The cost of peak load reduction for the Lower Midwest was $63 per kW, considerably less than the $150 per kW benchmark for cost-effectiveness. Utility companies in the Lower Midwest and throughout the country can invest in shade tree programs as a cost-effective energy conservation measure to lower peak energy demands.

Trees modify climate and conserve building energy use in three principal ways (fig. 3):

- Shading reduces the amount of heat absorbed and stored by built surfaces.
- **Evapotranspiration** converts liquid water to water vapor and thus cools the air by using solar energy that would otherwise result in heating of the air.
- Reducing windspeed reduces the infiltration of outside air into interior spaces and conductive heat loss, especially where conductivity is relatively high (e.g., glass windows) (Simpson 1998).

How trees work to save energy

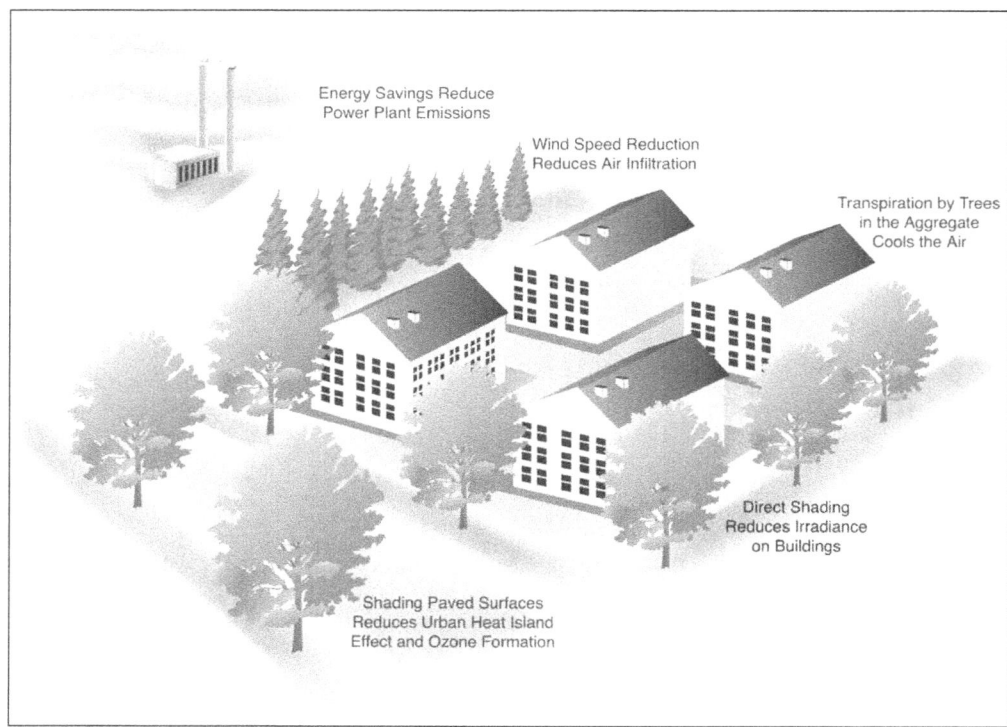

Figure 3—Trees save energy for heating and cooling by shading buildings, lowering summertime temperatures, and reducing windspeeds. Secondary benefits from energy conservation are reduced water consumption and reduced pollutant emissions by powerplants (drawing by Mike Thomas).

Trees lower temperatures

Summer temperatures in cities can be 3 to 8 °F warmer than temperatures in the surrounding countryside. This is known as the **urban heat island** effect. Trees and other vegetation can combat this warming effect at small and large scales. On individual building sites, trees may lower air temperatures up to 5 °F compared with outside the **greenspace**. At larger scales (6 mi^2), temperature differences of more than 9 °F have been observed between city centers and more vegetated suburban areas (Akbari et al. 1992). A recent study for New York City compared trees, living roofs, and light surfaces and found that street trees provide the "greatest cooling potential per unit area" (Rosenzweig et al. 2006).

Trees increase energy efficiency and save money

For individual buildings, strategically placed trees can increase energy efficiency in the summer and winter. Because the summer sun is low in the east and west for several hours each day, solar angles should be considered (fig. 4). Trees that shade east and, especially, west walls help keep buildings cool. In the winter, allowing sunlight to strike the southern side of a building can warm interior spaces.

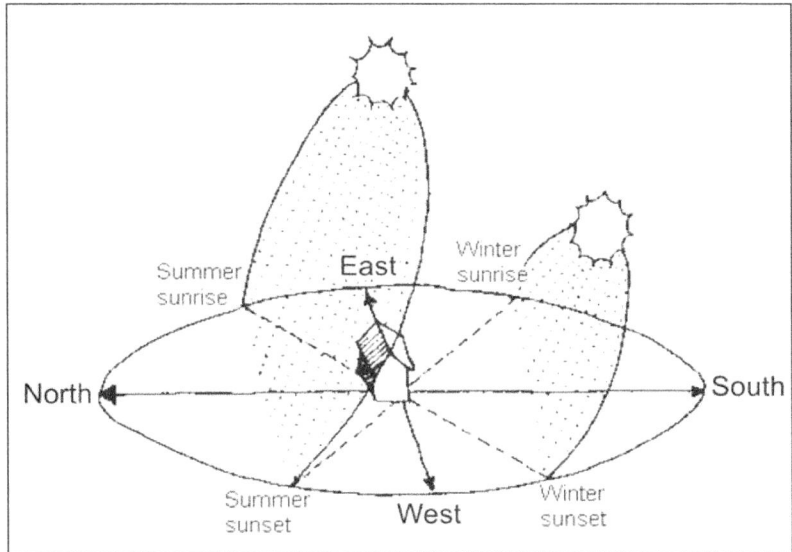

Figure 4—Paths of the sun on winter and summer solstices (from Sand 1991). Summer heat gain is primarily through east- and west-facing windows and walls. The roof receives most irradiance, but insulated attics reduce heat gain to living spaces. The winter sun, at a lower angle, strikes the south-facing surfaces.

However, the trunks and bare branches of **deciduous** trees that shade south- and east-facing walls during winter may increase heating costs by blocking 40 percent or more of winter sun (McPherson 1984).

Windbreaks reduce air infiltration and conductive heat loss from buildings. Rates at which outside air infiltrates a building can increase substantially with windspeed. In cold, windy weather, the entire volume of air, even in newer or tightly sealed homes, may change every 2 to 3 hours. Windbreaks can reduce windspeed and resulting air infiltration by up to 50 percent, translating into potential annual heating savings of 10 to 12 percent (Heisler 1986). Windspeed reductions also decrease heat transfer through windows, walls, and roofs by reducing the overall heat transfer coefficient for these surfaces. If located correctly, trees planted as windbreaks can also serve as living snowfences, storing and directing the movement of snow (for more information see Brandle and Nickerson 1996).

Trees provide greater energy savings in the Lower Midwest than in milder climate regions because they can have greater effects during the hot summers and cold winters. An average energy-efficient home in Rock Valley, Iowa, spends about $385 each year for heating and $115 for cooling. A computer simulation demonstrated that three 25-ft tall trees—two on the west side and one on the east side of the house—were estimated to save $9 each year for heating (2.5 MBtu) and $43 for cooling (940 kWh), a 10-percent reduction in annual heating and cooling costs (McPherson et al. 1993).

Conserving energy by greening our cities is important because it can be more cost-effective than building new powerplants (for more information, see the Center for Urban Forest Research's research summaries "Green Plants or Powerplants?" and "Save Dollars with Shade" [Geiger 2001, 2002a]). In the Lower Midwest region, there is ample opportunity to "retrofit" communities with more sustainable landscapes through strategic tree planting and care of existing trees.

Retrofit for more savings

Reducing Atmospheric Carbon Dioxide

Global temperatures have increased since the late 19th century, with major warming periods from 1910 to 1945 and from 1976 to the present (IPCC 2007). Human activities, primarily fossil fuel consumption, are adding greenhouse gases to the atmosphere, and current research suggests that the recent increases in temperature can be attributed in large part to increases in greenhouse gases (IPCC 2007). Higher global temperatures are expected to have a number of adverse effects, including increasing the number and extent of wildfires, an aspect of particular concern in parts of the Lower Midwest (McKenzie et al. 2004). Increasing frequency of extreme weather events will continue to tax emergency management resources.

Trees reduce CO_2

Urban forests have been recognized as important storage sites for carbon dioxide (CO_2), the primary greenhouse gas (Nowak and Crane 2002). Private markets dedicated to reducing CO_2 emissions by trading carbon credits are emerging (Chicago Climate Exchange 2007, CO2e.com 2007, McHale 2003). Carbon credits have sold for as much as EUR 33 per ton (about $52 at April 2008 exchange rates; European Climate Exchange 2006), and the social costs of CO_2 emissions (an estimate of the monetary value of worldwide damage done by CO_2 emissions from human activities) are estimated to range from £4 to £27 per ton ($14 to $54 per ton) (Pearce 2003). For comparison, for every $20 spent on a tree planting project in Arizona, 1 ton of atmospheric CO_2 was reduced (McPherson and Simpson 1999). As carbon trading markets become accredited and prices rise, these markets could provide monetary resources for community forestry programs.

Urban forests can reduce atmospheric CO_2 in two ways (fig. 5):

- Trees directly sequester CO_2 in their stems and leaves while they grow.
- Trees near buildings can reduce the demand for heating and air conditioning, thereby reducing emissions associated with power production.

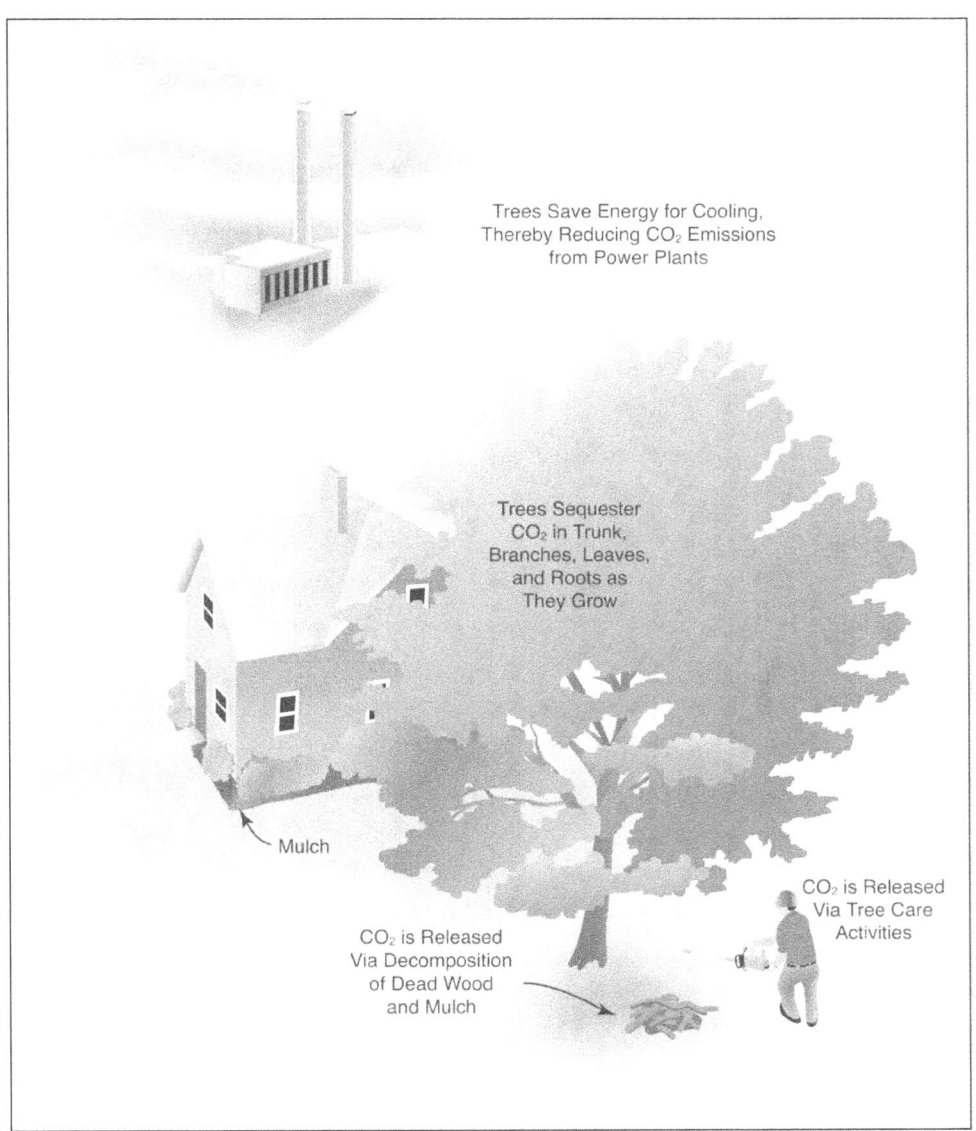

Figure 5—Trees sequester carbon dioxide (CO_2) as they grow and indirectly reduce CO_2 emissions from powerplants through energy conservation. At the same time, CO_2 is released through decomposition and tree care activities that involve fossil-fuel consumption (drawing by Mike Thomas).

At the same time, the positive impact of trees on CO_2 is offset by some emissions. To provide a complete picture of atmospheric CO_2 reductions from tree plantings, it is important to consider CO_2 released into the atmosphere through tree planting and care activities, as well as decomposition of wood from pruned or dead trees. During the process of planting and maintaining trees, vehicles, chain saws, chippers, and other equipment release CO_2 (fig. 5). Typically, CO_2 released from

Some tree-related activities release CO_2

Reduced CO_2 emissions

tree planting, maintenance, and other tree-related activities is about 2 to 8 percent of annual CO_2 reductions obtained through **sequestration** and **reduced power-plant emissions** (McPherson and Simpson 1999). And eventually, all trees die, and most of the carbon that has accumulated in their structure is released into the atmosphere as CO_2 through decomposition. The rate of release into the atmosphere depends on if and how the wood is reused. For instance, recycling of urban wood waste into products such as furniture can delay the rate of decomposition compared to its reuse as mulch. Tree waste can also be used as a fuel source to generate electricity. If this biomass fuel replaces a more carbon-intensive form of electricity production, there will be an overall reduction in atmospheric CO_2.

Regional variations in climate and the mix of fuels that produce energy to heat and cool buildings influence potential CO_2 emission reductions. The average emission rate in Indianapolis, Indiana, is 2,183 lb of CO_2 per **MWh** (US EPA 2006), a large amount, because 100 percent of Indianapolis's power is generated from fossil fuels like coal and natural gas. On the other hand, communities in other states like Illinois, have lower emission rates (average 1,155 lb of CO_2 per MWh) because nearly half of Illinois' power is nuclear-generated (US EPA 2006). Cities in the Lower Midwest with relatively high CO_2 emission rates will see greater benefits from reduced energy demand relative to other areas with lower emissions rates.

A study of the municipal trees of Indianapolis found that sequestrations and reduced emissions attributable to the 117,500 publicly owned trees equaled 16,344 tons of CO_2 (Peper et al. 2008) annually. Approximately 2,198 tons of CO_2 is released from decaying trees and during maintenance, with a positive net reduction in atmospheric CO_2 owing to trees of 14,146 tons.

Another study in Chicago focused on the carbon sequestration benefit of residential tree canopy. Tree **canopy cover** in two residential neighborhoods was estimated to sequester on average 0.112 lb/ft^2, and pruning activities released 0.016 lb/ft^2 (Jo and McPherson 1995). Net annual carbon uptake was 0.096 lb/ft^2.

CO_2 reduction through community forestry

Grass-roots tree-planting efforts to reduce atmospheric CO_2 can be very successful. Since 1990, Trees Forever, an Iowa-based nonprofit organization, has planted trees for energy savings and atmospheric CO_2 reduction with utility sponsorships. Over 1 million trees have been planted in 400 communities with the help of 120,000 volunteers. These trees are estimated to offset CO_2 emissions by 50,000 tons annually. Based on an Iowa State University study, survival rates are an amazing 91 percent indicating a highly trained and committed volunteer force (Ramsay 2002).

Improving Air Quality

Approximately 159 million people live in areas where **ozone** (O_3) concentrations violate federal air quality standards. About 100 million people live in areas where dust and other small particulate matter (PM_{10}) exceed levels for healthy air. Communities in Illinois, Indiana, and Ohio are among the cities previously listed in the U.S. EPAs (Environmental Protection Agency) Green Book (US EPA 2006) as being in violation of federal air quality standards for PM_{10} but are currently listed as maintenance areas (previously nonattainment areas), no longer in violation of federal air quality standards for PM_{10} or 8-hour ozone levels. Air pollution is a serious health threat to many city dwellers, causing asthma, coughing, headaches, respiratory and heart disease, and cancer (Smith 1990). Impaired health results in increased social costs for medical care, greater absenteeism, and reduced longevity.

Recently, the EPA recognized tree planting as a measure in state implementation plans for reducing O_3. Air quality management districts have funded tree planting projects to control PM_{10}. These policy decisions are creating new opportunities to plant and care for trees as a method for controlling air pollution (Luley and Bond 2002; for more information see www.treescleanair.org [USDA FS 2006b] and the Center for Urban Forest Research's research summary *Trees—The Air Pollution Solution* [Geiger 2006]).

Urban forests provide a number of air quality benefits:

- They absorb gaseous pollutants (e.g., O_3, nitrogen dioxide [NO_2], and sulfur dioxide [SO_2]) through leaf surfaces (fig. 6).
- They intercept PM_{10} (e.g., dust, ash, pollen, smoke) (fig. 6).
- They release oxygen through photosynthesis.
- They transpire water and shade surfaces, which lowers air temperatures, thereby reducing O_3 levels.
- They reduce energy use, which reduces emissions of pollutants from powerplants, including NO_2, SO_2, PM_{10}, and volatile organic compounds (VOCs) (fig. 6).
- They shade paved surfaces and parked cars, reducing hydrocarbon emissions (fig. 6).

Trees may also adversely affect air quality. Most trees emit **biogenic volatile organic compounds** (BVOCs) such as isoprenes and monoterpenes that can contribute to O_3 formation. The contribution of BVOC emissions from city trees to O_3 formation depends on complex geographic and atmospheric interactions that

Trees improve air quality

Trees affect ozone formation

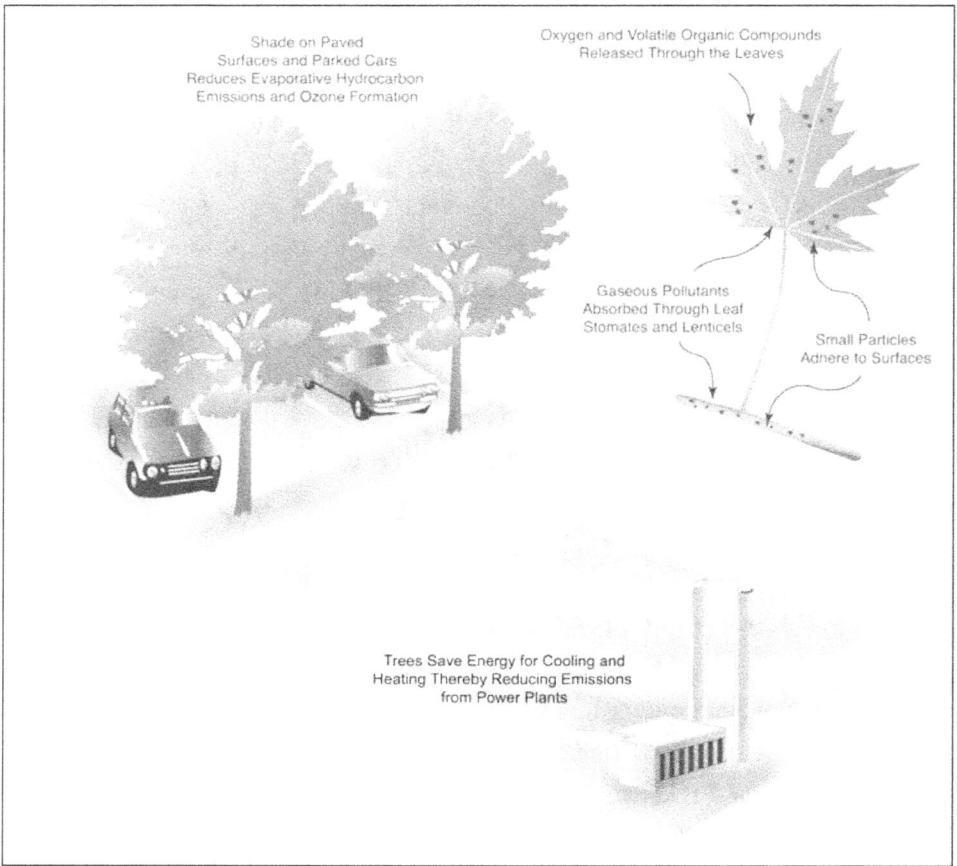

Figure 6—Trees absorb gaseous pollutants, retain particles on their surfaces, and release oxygen and volatile organic compounds. By cooling urban heat islands and shading parked cars, trees can reduce ozone formation (drawing by Mike Thomas).

have not been studied in most cities. Some complicating factors include variations with temperature and atmospheric levels of NO_2.

A computer simulation study for Atlanta suggested that it would be very difficult to meet EPA ozone standards in the region by using trees because of the high BVOC emissions from native pines and other vegetation (Chameides et al. 1988). The results, however, were not straightforward. A later study showed that although removing trees reduced BVOC emissions, any positive effect was overwhelmed by increased hydrocarbon emissions from natural and anthropogenic sources owing to the increased air temperatures associated with tree removal (Cardelino and Chameides 1990). A similar finding was reported for the Houston-Galveston area, where deforestation associated with urbanization from 1992 to 2000 increased surface temperatures. Despite the decrease in BVOC emissions, O_3 concentrations increased because of the enhanced urban heat island effect during simulated episodes (Kim et al. 2005).

As well, the O_3-forming potential of tree species differs considerably (Benjamin and Winer 1998). Trees emitting the greatest relative amount of BVOCs are sweetgum, blackgum, sycamore, poplar, and oak (Nowak 2000). In a study in the Los Angeles basin, increased planting of low-BVOC-emitting tree species was shown to reduce O_3 concentrations, whereas planting of medium and high emitters would increase overall O_3 concentrations (Taha 1996). A study in the Northeastern United States, however, found that species mix had no detectable effects on O_3 concentrations (Nowak et al. 2000). Although new trees increased BVOC emissions, ambient VOC emissions were so high that additional BVOCs had little effect on air quality. These potentially negative effects of trees on one kind of air pollution must be considered in light of their great benefit in other areas.

Trees absorb gaseous pollutants through stomates, tiny openings in the leaves. Other methods of pollutant removal include adsorption of gases to plant surfaces and uptake through bark pores. Once gases enter the leaf, they diffuse into intercellular spaces, where some react with inner leaf surfaces and others are absorbed by water films to form acids. Pollutants can damage plants by altering their metabolism and growth. At high concentrations, pollutants cause visible damage to leaves, such as spotting and bleaching (Costello and Jones 2003). Although some pollutants may pose health hazards to plants, pollutants such as nitrogenous gases can also be sources of essential nutrients for them.

Trees intercept small airborne particles. Some particles that are intercepted by a tree are absorbed, but most adhere to plant surfaces. Species with hairy or rough leaf, twig, and bark surfaces are efficient interceptors (Smith and Dochinger 1976). Intercepted particles are often resuspended to the atmosphere when wind blows the branches, and rain will wash some particulates off plant surfaces. The ultimate fate of these pollutants depends on whether they fall onto paved surfaces and enter the stormwater system, or fall on pervious surfaces, where they are filtered in the soil.

Urban forests clean the air we breathe by releasing oxygen as a byproduct of photosynthesis. Net annual oxygen production varies depending on tree species, size, health, and location. A typical person consumes 675 lb of oxygen per year (Perry and LeVan 2003). Urban forests in the United States are estimated currently to produce 67 million tons of oxygen annually, enough oxygen to offset human oxygen consumption for about two-thirds of the U.S. population (Nowak et al. 2007).

**Trees absorb
gaseous pollutants**

**Trees intercept
particulate matter**

Trees near buildings can reduce the demand for heating and air conditioning, thereby reducing emissions of PM_{10}, SO_2, NO_2, and VOCs associated with electric power production, an effect that can be sizable. For example, a strategically located tree can save 100 kWh in electricity for cooling annually (McPherson and Simpson 1999, 2002, 2003). Assuming that this conserved electricity comes from a typical new coal-fired powerplant in the Lower Midwest, the tree reduces emissions of SO_2 by 1.25 lb, NO_2 by 0.39 lb (US EPA 2003), and PM_{10} by 0.84 lb (US EPA 1998). The same tree is responsible for conserving 60 gal of water in cooling towers and reducing annual CO_2 emissions by 200 lb.

In Fayetteville, Arkansas, the tree **canopy** over nearly 29,000 acres was estimated to remove 731,000 lb of air pollutants annually with a value of $1.6 million (American Forests 2002). The area experienced a substantial 18 percent decline in heavy canopy cover between 1985 and 2000 owing to increased development. If the loss in canopy continues at its current 18 percent rate, estimates are that air quality benefits will be reduced to $1.3 million and carbon storage will decline from 330,000 to 273,000 thousand tons. Chicago's 50.8 million trees were estimated to remove 234 tons of PM_{10}, 210 tons of O_3, 93 tons of SO_2, and 17 tons of carbon monoxide in 1991. This environmental service was valued at $9.2 million (Nowak 1994).

Trees in a Davis, California, parking lot were found to improve air quality by reducing air temperatures 1 to 3 °F (Scott et al. 1999). By shading asphalt surfaces and parked vehicles, trees reduce hydrocarbon emissions (VOCs) from gasoline that evaporates out of leaky fuel tanks and worn hoses (for more information, see our research summary *Where Are All the Cool Parking Lots?* [Geiger 2002b]). These evaporative emissions are a principal component of smog, and parked vehicles are a primary source (fig. 7). In California, parking-lot tree plantings can be funded as an air quality improvement measure because of the associated reductions in evaporative emissions.

Tree shade prevents evaporative hydrocarbon emissions

Reducing Stormwater Runoff and Improving Hydrology

Urban stormwater runoff is a major source of pollution entering wetlands, streams, lakes, and oceans. Healthy trees can reduce the amount of runoff and pollutants in receiving waters (Cappiella et al. 2005). This is important because federal law requires states and localities to control nonpoint-source pollution, such as runoff from pavements, buildings, and landscapes. Trees are mini-reservoirs, controlling runoff at the source, thereby reducing runoff volumes and erosion of watercourses,

Figure 7—Trees planted to shade parking areas can reduce hydrocarbon emissions and improve air quality.

as well as delaying the onset of **peak flows**. Trees can reduce runoff in several ways (fig. 8; for more information, see our research summary *Is All Your Rain Going Down the Drain?* [Geiger 2003]):

- Leaves and branch surfaces intercept and store rainfall, thereby reducing runoff volumes and delaying the onset of peak flows.
- Roots reduce soil compaction, increasing the rate at which rainfall infiltrates soil and the capacity of soil to store water, reducing overland flow.
- Tree canopies reduce soil erosion by diminishing the impact of raindrops on barren surfaces.
- **Transpiration** through tree leaves reduces moisture levels in the soil, increasing the soil's capacity to store rainfall.

Rainfall that is stored temporarily on canopy leaf and bark surfaces is called intercepted rainfall. Intercepted water evaporates, drips from leaf surfaces, and flows down stem surfaces to the ground. Tree surface saturation generally occurs after 1 to 2 in of rain has fallen (Xiao et al. 2000). During large storm events, rainfall exceeds the amount that the tree **crown** can store, about 50 to 100 gal per tree.

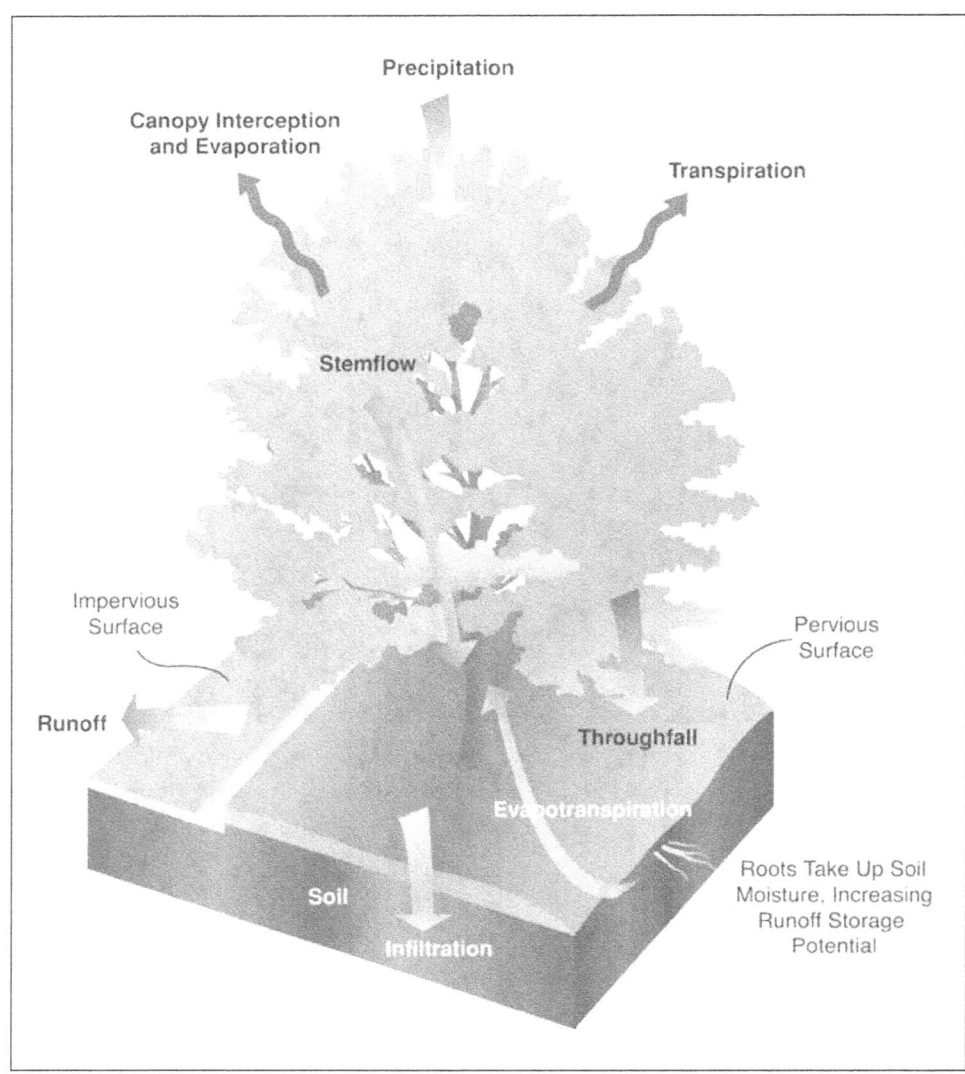

Figure 8—Trees intercept a portion of rainfall that evaporates and never reaches the ground. Some rainfall runs to the ground along branches and stems (stemflow), and some falls through gaps or drips off leaves and branches (throughfall). Transpiration increases soil moisture storage potential (drawing by Mike Thomas).

Trees reduce runoff

The **interception** benefit is the amount of rainfall that does not reach the ground because it evaporates from the crown. As a result, the volume of runoff is reduced and the time of peak flow is delayed. Trees protect water quality by substantially reducing runoff during small rainfall events that are responsible for most pollutant washoff. Therefore, urban forests generally produce more benefits through water quality protection than through flood control (Xiao et al. 1998, 2000).

The amount of rainfall trees intercept depends on their architecture, rainfall patterns, and climate. Tree-crown characteristics that influence interception are the trunk, stem, and surface areas, textures, area of gaps, period when leaves are present, and dimensions (e.g., tree height and diameter). Trees with coarse surfaces retain more rainfall than those with smooth surfaces. Large trees generally intercept more rainfall than small trees do because greater surface areas allow for greater evaporation rates. Tree crowns with few gaps reduce **throughfall** to the ground. Species that are in leaf when rainfall is plentiful are more effective than deciduous species that have dropped their leaves during the rainy season.

Studies that have simulated urban forest effects on stormwater runoff have reported reductions of 2 to 7 percent. Annual interception of rainfall by Sacramento's urban forest for the total urbanized area was only about 2 percent because of the winter rainfall pattern and sparsity of **evergreen** species (Xiao et al. 1998). However, average interception in canopied areas ranged from 6 to 13 percent (150 gal per tree), similar to values reported for rural forests. Broadleaf evergreens and **conifers** intercept more rainfall than deciduous species in areas where rainfall is highest in fall, winter, or spring (Xiao and McPherson 2002).

In Albuquerque, a city with approximately one-quarter the rainfall of the Lower Midwest region, the canopy of the 21,000 municipal park trees reduced runoff by more than 11 million gal, with an estimated value of $56,000 (Vargas et al. 2006). In contrast, in Montgomery, Alabama, a city with about half as many people but many more trees and approximately 50 in more rain than Albuquerque, the tree canopy was estimated to reduce runoff by 1.7 billion gal, valued at $454 million per 20-year construction cycle (American Forests 2004). According to a recent study, the 117,500 municipal trees of Indianapolis, Indiana, were estimated to intercept approximately 319 million gal of stormwater annually, with an estimated value of $1.9 million (Peper et al. 2008).

Urban forests can provide other hydrologic benefits, too. For example, tree plantations, nurseries, or landscapes can be irrigated with partially treated wastewater. Infiltration of water through the soil can be a safe and productive means of water treatment. Reused wastewater applied to urban forest lands can recharge aquifers, reduce stormwater-treatment loads, and create income through sales of nursery or wood products. Recycling urban wastewater into greenspace areas can be an economical means of treatment and disposal while at the same time providing other environmental benefits (USDA NRCS 2005).

Aesthetics and Other Benefits

Trees provide a host of aesthetic, social, economic, and health benefits that should be included in any benefit-cost analysis. One of the most frequently cited reasons

Urban forests can treat wastewater

For beautification

Attractiveness of retail settings

Public safety benefits

Property value benefits

that people plant trees is for beautification. Trees add color, texture, line, and form to the landscape, softening the hard geometry that dominates built environments. Research on the aesthetic quality of residential streets has shown that street trees are the single strongest positive influence on scenic quality (Schroeder and Cannon 1983).

In surveys, consumers have shown greater preference for commercial streetscapes with trees. In contrast to areas without trees, shoppers shop more often and longer in well-landscaped business districts. They are willing to pay more for parking and up to 11 percent more for goods and services (Wolf 1999).

Research in public housing complexes found that outdoor spaces with trees were used significantly more often than spaces without trees. By facilitating interactions among residents, trees can contribute to reduced levels of domestic violence, as well as foster safer and more sociable neighborhood environments (Sullivan and Kuo 1996).

Well-maintained trees increase the "curb appeal" of properties (fig. 9). Research documenting the increase in dollar value that can be attributed to trees is difficult to conduct and is still in early stages, but some studies comparing sales

Figure 9—Trees beautify a neighborhood, increasing property values and creating a more sociable environment.

prices of residential properties having different numbers of trees have suggested that people are willing to pay 3 to 7 percent more for properties with ample trees versus few or no trees. One of the most comprehensive studies of the influence of trees on home property values was based on actual sales prices and found that each large front-yard tree was associated with about a 1-percent increase in sales price (Anderson and Cordell 1988). A much greater value of 9 percent ($15,000) was determined in a U.S. Tax Court case for the loss of a large black oak on a property valued at $164,500 (Neely 1988). Depending on average home sales prices, the value of this benefit can contribute significantly to cities' property tax revenues.

Social and psycho-logical benefits

Scientific studies confirm that trees in cities provide social and psychological benefits. Humans derive substantial pleasure from trees, whether it is inspiration from their beauty, a spiritual connection, or a sense of meaning (Dwyer et al. 1992, Lewis 1996). After natural disasters, people often report a sense of loss if their community forest has been damaged (Hull 1992). Views of trees and nature from homes and offices provide restorative experiences that ease mental fatigue and help people to concentrate (Kaplan and Kaplan 1989). Desk workers with a view of nature report lower rates of sickness and greater satisfaction with their jobs compared to those having no visual connection to nature (Kaplan 1992). Trees provide important settings for recreation and relaxation in and near cities. The act of planting trees can have social value, as bonds between people and local groups often result.

Human health benefits

A series of studies on human stress caused by general urban conditions shows that views of nature reduce the stress response of both body and mind (Parsons et al. 1998), improving general well-being. Urban green also appears to have a positive effect on the human immune system. Hospitalized patients who have views of nature and spend time outdoors need less medication, sleep better, have a better outlook, and recover more quickly than patients without connections to nature (Ulrich 1985). Skin cancer is a particular concern in the sunny Lower Midwest region. Shade from trees reduces exposure to ultraviolet (UV) light, thereby lowering the risk of harmful effects from skin cancer and cataracts (Tretheway and Manthe 1999). At the latitudes of the Lower Midwest, the ultraviolet protection factor provided by trees increases from approximately 2 under a 30-percent canopy cover to approximately 15 under a 90-percent canopy cover (Grant et al. 2002). Because early exposure to UV radiation is a risk factor for later development of skin cancer, planting trees around playgrounds, schools, day care centers, and ball fields can be especially valuable in helping reduce the risk of later-life cancers.

Noise reduction

Certain environmental benefits from trees are more difficult to quantify than those previously described, but can be just as important. Noise can reach unhealthy levels in cities. Trucks, trains, and planes can produce noise that exceeds 100 decibels (dB), twice the level at which noise becomes a health risk. Thick strips of vegetation in conjunction with landforms or solid barriers can reduce some highway noise and have a psychological effect (Cook 1978), but if vegetation is used as the only sound barrier, the amount necessary to achieve measurable reductions in noise (about 200 ft for a 10-dB reduction) may be impractical (U.S. Department of Transportation 1995). Other studies have shown that the performance of noise barriers is increased when used in combination with vegetative screens (van Rentergehm et al. 2002).

Wildlife habitats

Numerous types of wildlife inhabit cities and are generally highly valued by residents. For example, older parks, cemeteries, and botanical gardens often contain a rich assemblage of wildlife. Remnant woodlands and **riparian habitats** within cities can connect a city to its surrounding bioregion (fig. 10). Wetlands, greenways (linear parks), and other greenspace can provide habitats that conserve **biodiversity** (Platt et al. 1994).

Urban forestry can provide jobs for both skilled and unskilled labor. Public service programs and grassroots-led urban and community forestry programs

Figure 10—Natural areas within cities are refuges for wildlife and help connect city dwellers with their ecosystems.

provide horticultural training to volunteers across the United States. Also, urban and community forestry provides educational opportunities for residents who want to learn about nature through firsthand experience (McPherson and Mathis 1999). Local nonprofit tree groups and municipal volunteer programs often provide educational material and hands-on training in the care of trees and work with area schools.

Tree shade on streets can help offset the cost of managing pavement by protecting it from weathering. The asphalt paving on streets contains stone aggregate in an oil binder. Tree shade lowers the street surface temperature, thereby reducing heating and volatilization of the binder (McPherson and Muchnick 2005). As a result, the aggregate remains protected for a longer period by the oil binder. When unprotected, vehicles loosen the aggregate, and much like sandpaper, the loose aggregate grinds down the pavement. Because most weathering of asphalt-concrete pavement occurs during the first 5 to 10 years when new street tree plantings provide little shade, this benefit mainly applies when older streets are resurfaced (fig. 11). In snowier communities, the benefit from summer shade can be offset by winter shade that prolongs snow and ice accumulation, and may result in greater

Jobs and environmental education

Shade can reduce street maintenance

Figure 11—Although shade trees can be expensive to maintain, their shade can reduce the costs of resurfacing streets (McPherson and Muchnick 2005), promote pedestrian travel, and improve air quality directly through pollutant uptake and indirectly through reduced emissions of volatile organic compounds from cars.

use of salt and sand. Further study is needed to evaluate the seasonal effects of tree shade on paving condition and safety.

Costs

The environmental, social, and economic benefits of urban and community forests come, of course, at a price. A national survey reported that communities in the Lower Midwest region spent an average of about $1.94 per tree, in 1994, for street- and park-tree management (Tschantz and Sacamano 1994). This amount is relatively low, with only two national regions spending less than this and eight regions spending more. Nationwide, the single largest expenditure was for tree pruning, followed by tree removal/disposal, and tree planting. The survey did not include non-tree-care costs, such as money spent on infrastructure repair, litigation, and cleanup.

Municipal costs of tree care

Our survey of **municipal foresters** in Carmel, Terre Haute, and Indianapolis, Indiana, and Cincinnati and Marietta, Ohio, indicates that they are spending about $20 per tree annually. The greatest costs are for pruning ($5 to $8 per tree) and administration and inspection ($4 to $6 per tree). Planting ($4 per tree) and removal and disposal ($2 to $3 per tree) are the next most costly.

Residential costs differ

Annual expenditures for tree management on private property have not been well documented. Costs differ considerably, ranging from some commercial or residential properties that receive regular professional landscape service to others that are virtually "wild" and without maintenance. Our survey of commercial arborists in the Lower Midwest indicated that expenditures typically range from $9 to $13 per tree. Expenditures are usually greatest for pruning, planting, and removal.

Planting and Maintaining Trees

Planting costs include the cost of the tree and the cost for planting, staking, and mulching. Based on our survey of Lower Midwest municipal and commercial arborists, planting costs differ with tree size and range from $106 for a 2-in **diameter at breast height** (4.5 ft; **d.b.h.**) tree to $550 for a 5-in d.b.h. tree. Pruning cycles differ by city and by tree size and range from once every 2 to 5 years for new trees to once in 7 to 10 years for large, mature trees. However, there are cities where pruning is conducted on an as-needed or reactive basis. The cost for pruning young trees ranged from $10 to $20 for a public tree and from $50 to $70 for a yard tree; the cost to prune a large, mature tree was about $180 for public trees and ranged from $230 to $900 for yard trees.

Because of the region's rainy, humid summer climate, most trees do not require irrigation throughout their lives, and because most are planted in areas that are already irrigated, such as parkways or other landscaped areas, the cost for additional water for the trees is negligible and is ignored for the purposes of this guide. Newly planted trees, however, require additional watering at least for the first year to successfully establish. The costs of irrigation for public trees are estimated at about $1.75 for the first 5 years, mainly for the labor costs involved in visiting the trees with a water truck or other time-intensive methods. No additional costs are included for establishment watering of yard trees, as the few minutes of labor necessary are considered negligible.

At the end of a tree's life, removal costs can be substantial, especially for large trees. Removal and disposal of small trees (under 3 in d.b.h.) cost between $10 and $50, but a large tree may cost several thousand dollars to remove. According to our survey, total costs for removal of trees and stumps are approximately $26 to $62 per in d.b.h. for yard trees and $19 to $33 per in d.b.h. for public trees.

Conflicts With Urban Infrastructure

Like other cities across the United States, communities in the Lower Midwest region are spending millions of dollars each year to manage conflicts between trees and power lines, sidewalks, sewers, and other elements of the urban infrastructure. According to our survey, cities in the region are spending about $1 to $2 per tree annually on sidewalk, curb, and gutter repair costs. This amount is far less than the $11.22 per tree reported for 18 California cities (McPherson 2000). In addition, the figures for California apply only to street trees and do not include repair costs for damaged sewer lines, building foundations, parking lots, and various other **hardscape** elements.

In some cities, decreasing budgets are increasing the sidewalk-repair backlog and forcing cities to shift the costs of sidewalk repair to residents. This shift has significant impacts on residents in older areas, where large trees have outgrown small sites and infrastructure has deteriorated. It should be noted that trees are not always fully responsible for these problems. In older areas, in particular, sidewalks and curbs may have reached the end of their 20- to 25-year service life, or may have been poorly constructed in the first place (Sydnor et al. 2000).

Efforts to control the costs of these conflicts are having alarming effects on urban forests (Bernhardt and Swiecki 1993, Thompson and Ahern 2000):

Tree roots can damage sidewalks

Costs of conflicts

- Cities are downsizing their urban forests by planting smaller trees. Although small trees are appropriate under power lines and in small planting sites, they are less effective than large trees at providing shade, absorbing air pollutants, and intercepting rainfall.
- Thousands of healthy urban trees are lost each year and their benefits forgone because of sidewalk damage, the second most common reason that street and park trees were removed.
- Most cities surveyed were removing more trees than they were planting. Residents forced to pay for sidewalk repairs may not want replacement trees.

Cost-effective strategies to retain benefits from large street trees while reducing costs associated with infrastructure conflicts are described in *Reducing Infrastructure Damage by Tree Roots* (Costello and Jones 2003). Matching the growth characteristics of trees to the conditions at the planting site is one important strategy.

Cleaningup after trees

Tree roots can also damage old sewer lines that are cracked or otherwise susceptible to invasion. Sewer repair companies estimate that sewer damage is minor until trees and sewers are over 30 years old, and roots from trees in yards are usually more of a problem than roots from trees in planter strips along streets. The latter assertion may be because the sewers are closer to the root zone as they enter houses than at the street. Repair costs typically range from $100 for sewer rodding (inserting a cleaning implement to temporarily remove roots) to $1,000 or more for sewer excavation and replacement.

Most communities sweep their streets regularly to reduce surface-runoff pollution entering local waterways. Street trees drop leaves, flowers, fruit, and branches year round that constitute a significant portion of debris collected from city streets. When leaves fall and rains begin, **tree litter** can clog sewers, dry wells, and other elements of flood-control systems. Costs include additional labor needed to remove leaves, and property damage caused by localized flooding. Wind and ice storms also incur cleanup costs.

The cost of addressing conflicts between trees and power lines is reflected in electric rates. Large trees under power lines require more frequent pruning than better suited trees, which can make large trees appear less attractive (fig. 12). Frequent crown reduction reduces the benefits these trees could otherwise provide. Moreover, increased costs for pruning are passed on to customers.

Figure 12—Large trees planted under power lines can require extensive pruning, which increases tree care costs and reduces the benefits of those trees, including their appearance. The use of small trees, like those shown here, will reduce pruning costs and maintain benefits.

Wood Salvage, Recycling, and Disposal

According to our survey, many Lower Midwest cities are recycling green waste from urban trees as firewood, mulch, and compost. Some powerplants will use this wood to generate electricity, thereby helping defray costs for hauling and grinding. Generally, the net costs of waste-wood disposal are less than 1 percent of total tree care costs, and cities and contractors may break even. The cost of wood disposal may be higher depending on geographic location and the presence of exotic pests that require special waste-wood disposal processes. In some cities within the region, income from sales of firewood, mulch, and compost exceeds the cost of hauling and disposal. For example, Indianapolis chips 84 percent of its tree removals for use by the city and partners as mulch. Savings to the city exceed the cost of mulching by $30 per ton.

Recycling green waste may pay for itself

Chapter 3. Benefits and Costs of Community Forests in Lower Midwest Communities

This chapter presents estimated benefits and costs for trees planted in typical residential yards and public sites. Because benefits and costs differ with tree size, we report results for representative small, medium, and large deciduous trees and for a representative conifer.

Estimates are initial approximations, as some benefits and costs are intangible or difficult to quantify (e.g., impacts on psychological health, crime, and violence). Limited knowledge about physical processes at work and their interactions makes estimates imprecise (e.g., fate of air pollutants trapped by trees and then washed to the ground by rainfall). Tree growth and mortality rates are highly variable throughout the region. Benefits and costs also differ, depending on differences in climate, pollutant concentrations, maintenance practices, and other factors. Given the Lower Midwest region's diverse landscape, with different climates, soils, and types of community forestry programs, the approach used here provides first-order approximations. It is a general accounting that can be easily adapted and adjusted for local planting projects. It provides a basis for decisions that set priorities and influence management direction (Maco and McPherson 2003).

Overview of Procedures
Approach

In this study, annual benefits and costs are estimated over a 40-year planning horizon for newly planted trees in three residential yard locations (east, south, and west of the residence) and a public streetside or park location (app. 2). Henceforth, we refer to trees in these hypothetical locations as "yard" trees and "public" trees, respectively. Prices are assigned to each cost (e.g., planting, pruning, removal, irrigation, infrastructure repair, liability) and benefit (e.g., heating/cooling energy savings, air pollutant mitigation, stormwater runoff reduction, and aesthetic and other benefits measured as increases in property value) through direct estimation and implied valuation of benefits as environmental externalities. This approach makes it possible to estimate the net benefits of plantings in "typical" locations by using "typical" tree species. More information on data collection, modeling procedures, and assumptions can be found in appendix 3.

Tree care costs based on survey findings

Tree benefits based on numerial models

Tree mortality included

To account for differences in the mature size and growth of different tree species, we report results for a small (eastern redbud), medium (littleleaf linden), and large (northern hackberry) deciduous tree (figs. 13 to 16) (see "Common and Scientific Names" section). Tree dimensions are derived from growth curves developed from street trees in Indianapolis, Indiana (Peper et al. 2008) (fig. 16). The selection of these species is based on data availability and representative growth and is not intended to endorse their use in large numbers. Relying on too few species can increase the likelihood of catastrophic loss owing to pests, disease, or other threat.

Frequency and costs of tree management are estimated based on surveys with municipal foresters from Carmel, Indianapolis, and Terre Haute, Indiana, and Cincinnati and Marietta, Ohio. In addition, several commercial arborists from Brownsburg, Carmel, and Indianapolis, Indiana, and Gallipolis and Columbus, Ohio, provided information on tree management costs on residential properties.

Benefits are calculated with numerical models and data both from the region (e.g., pollutant emission factors for avoided emissions from energy savings) and from local sources (e.g., Indianapolis climate data for energy effects). Regional electricity and natural gas prices are used in this study to quantify energy savings. **Damage costs** and **control costs** are used to estimate **willingness to pay.** For example, the value of stormwater runoff reduction owing to rainfall interception by trees is estimated by using marginal control costs. If a community or developer is willing to pay an average of $0.01 per gal of treated and controlled runoff to meet minimum standards, then the stormwater runoff mitigation value of a tree that intercepts 1,000 gal of rainfall, eliminating the need for control, should be $10.

Reporting Results

Results are reported in terms of annual value per tree planted. To make these calculations realistic, however, mortality rates are included. Based on our survey of regional municipal foresters and commercial arborists, this analysis assumes that 50 percent of the planted trees will die over the 40-year period. Annual mortality rates are 2 percent per year for the first 5 years and 1.4 percent per year for the remainder of the 40-year period. This accounting approach "grows" trees in different locations and uses computer simulation to calculate the annual flow of benefits and costs as trees mature and die (McPherson 1992). In appendix 2, results are reported at 5-year intervals for 40 years.

Figure 13—The eastern redbud represents small trees in this guide.

Figure 14—The littleleaf linden represents medium trees in this guide.

Figure 15—The northern hackberry represents large trees in this guide.

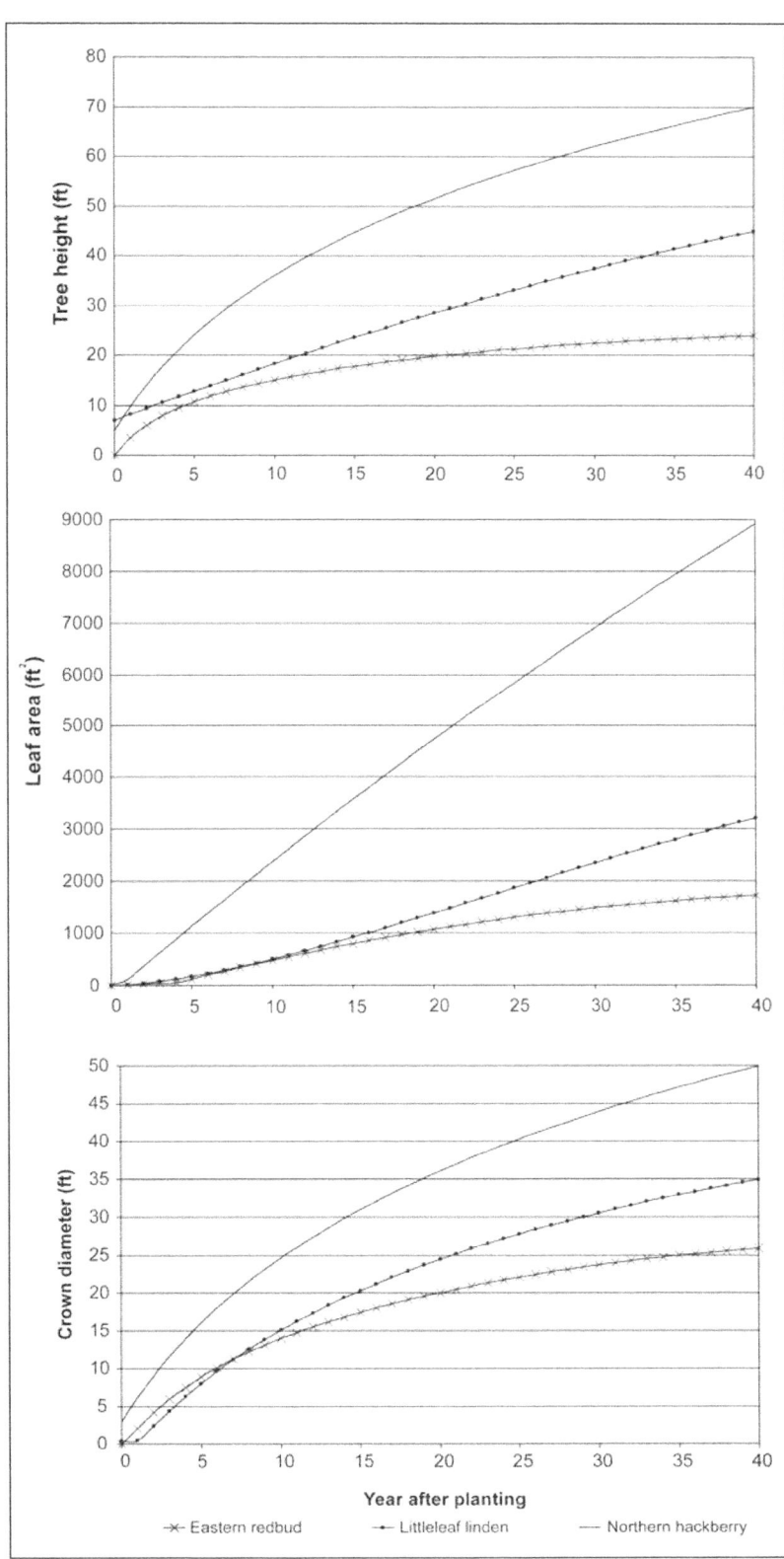

Figure 16—Tree growth curves are based on data collected from street trees in Indianapolis, Indiana. Data for representa-tive small, medium, and large trees are for the eastern redbud, littleleaf linden, and northern hackberry, respectively. Differences in leaf surface area among species are most important for this analysis because functional benefits such as summer shade, rainfall interception, and pollutant uptake are related to leaf area.

Findings of This Study

Average Annual Net Benefits

Average annual net benefits (benefits minus costs) per tree over a 40-year period increase with mature tree size (for detailed results see app. 2):

- $4 to $12 for a small tree
- $12 to $24 for a medium tree
- $47 to $60 for a large tree

Large trees provide greater benefits

Our findings demonstrate that average annual net benefits from large trees like the hackberry are substantially greater than those from small trees like the eastern redbud. Average annual net benefits for the small, medium, and large deciduous public trees are $3, $11, and $43, respectively. The largest average annual net benefits, however, stem from yard trees opposite the west-facing wall of a house: $12, $24, and $60, for small, medium, and large deciduous trees, respectively.

Net annual benefits at year 40

At year 40, the large yard tree opposite a west wall produces a net annual benefit of $80. In the same location, 40 years after planting, the eastern redbud and littleleaf linden produce annual net benefits of $14 and $32. Forty years after planting at a typical public site, the small, medium, and large deciduous trees provide annual net benefits of $4, $17, and $64, respectively.

Net benefits for a yard tree opposite a west house wall and a public tree also increase with size when summed over the entire 40-year period:

Net benefits summed over 40 years

- $475 (yard) and $149 (public) for a small tree
- $923 (yard) and $454 (public) for a medium tree
- $2,356 (yard) and $1,809 (public) for a large tree

Twenty years after planting, average annual benefits for all trees exceed costs of tree planting and management (tables 1 and 2). For a large hackberry in a yard 20 years after planting, the total value of environmental benefits alone ($51) is over six times the total annual cost ($8). Environmental benefits total $14 and $22, respectively, for the eastern redbud and littleleaf linden, and tree care costs are $3 and $7, respectively. Adding the value of aesthetics and other benefits to the environmental benefits results in even greater net benefits.

Year 20: environmental benefits exceed tree care costs

Net benefits for public trees at 20 years ($10, $18, and $57 for small, medium, and large deciduous trees, respectively; table 2) are less than yard trees ($19, $29, and $70) for two main reasons: public tree care costs are greater because public trees generally receive more intensive care than private trees; and energy benefits are lower for public trees than for yard trees because public trees are assumed to provide general climate effects, but not to shade buildings directly.

Table 1—Estimated annual benefits and costs for a private tree (residential yard) opposite the west-facing wall 20 years after planting

Benefit category	Eastern redbud small tree 20 ft tall 20-ft spread LSA = 1,056 ft²		Littleleaf linden medium tree 29 ft tall 24-ft spread LSA = 1,414 ft²		Northern hackberry large tree 51 ft tall 36-ft spread LSA = 4,718 ft²	
	Resource units	Total value	Resource units	Total value	Resource units	Total value
		Dollars		*Dollars*		*Dollars*
Electricity savings ($0.0680/kWh)	72 kWh	4.93	122 kWh	8.30	247 kWh	16.79
Natural gas savings ($0.97/therm)	-0.15 therms	-0.14	0.26 therms	0.25	0.20 therms	0.20
Carbon dioxide ($0.00334/lb)	171 lb	0.57	296 lb	0.99	653 lb	2.18
Ozone ($0.82/lb)	0.19 lb	0.16	0.29 lb	0.24	0.62 lb	0.51
Nitrogen dioxide ($0.82/lb)	0.17 lb	0.14	0.28 lb	0.23	0.59 lb	0.49
Sulfur dioxide ($1.50 /lb)	0.57 lb	0.86	0.93 lb	1.40	2.01 lb	3.02
Small particulate matter ($0.99/lb)	0.19 lb	0.19	0.25 lb	0.25	0.39 lb	0.39
Volatile organic compounds ($0.30/lb)	0.00 lb	0.01	0.07 lb	0.02	0.16 lb	0.05
Biogenic volatile organic compounds ($0.30/lb)	0 lb	0	-0.17 lb	-0.05	0 lb	0
Rainfall interception ($0.006/gal)	1,101 gal	6.83	1,644 gal	10.19	4,390 gal	27.22
Environmental subtotal		13.53		21.82		50.84
Other benefits		7.95		14.80		26.59
Total benefits		21.48		36.61		77.43
Total costs		2.86		7.40		7.65
Net benefits		18.63		29.22		69.78

LSA = leaf surface area.

Table 2—Estimated annual benefits and costs for a public tree (street/park) 20 years after planting

Benefit category	Eastern redbud small tree 20 ft tall 20-ft spread LSA = 1,056 ft^2		Littleleaf linden medium tree 29 ft tall 24-ft spread LSA = 1,414 ft^2		Northern hackberry large tree 51 ft tall 36-ft spread LSA = 4,718 ft^2	
	Resource units	Total value	Resource units	Total value	Resource units	Total value
		Dollars		*Dollars*		*Dollars*
Electricity savings ($0.0680/kWh)	31 kWh	2.12	47 kWh	3.23	103 kWh	7.03
Natural gas savings ($0.97/therm)	2 therms	1.62	2 therms	2.33	5 therms	4.56
Carbon dioxide ($0.00334/lb)	102.39 lb	0.34	158.52 lb	0.53	392.84 lb	1.31
Ozone ($0.82/lb)	0.19 lb	0.16	0.29 lb	0.24	0.62 lb	0.51
Nitrogen dioxide ($0.82/lb)	0.17 lb	0.14	0.28 lb	0.23	0.59 lb	0.49
Sulfur dioxide ($1.50 /lb)	0.57 lb	0.86	0.93 lb	1.40	2.01 lb	3.02
Small particulate matter ($0.99/lb)	0.19 lb	0.19	0.25 lb	0.25	0.39 lb	0.39
Volatile organic compounds ($0.30/lb)	0.04 lb	0.01	0.07 lb	0.02	0.16 lb	0.05
Biogenic volatile organic compounds ($0.30/lb)	0 lb	0.00	0 lb	-0.05	0 lb	0.00
Rainfall interception ($0.006/gal)	1,101 gal	6.83	1,644 gal	10.19	4,390 gal	27.22
Environmental subtotal		12.26		18.37		44.57
Other benefits		8.97		16.69		29.98
Total benefits		21.23		35.06		74.55
Total costs		11.17		16.82		17.71
Net benefits		10.06		18.23		56.85

LSA = leaf surface area.

Average Annual Costs

Averaged over 40 years, the costs for yard and public trees, respectively, are as follows:

- $9 and $16 for a small tree
- $10 and $18 for a medium tree
- $13 and $24 for a large tree

Annualized over the 40-year period, tree planting is the single greatest cost for yard trees, averaging $4 per tree per year (see app. 2 tables 7, 10, 13). Based on our survey, we assume in this study that a 2-in diameter at breast height (d.b.h.) yard tree is planted at a cost of $160. The cost for planting a 2-in d.b.h. public tree is $155. For public trees, where safety is particularly important and conflicts with infrastructure are greater, pruning is the greatest cost, with average annual costs of $5 to $8. Comparatively, annual pruning costs for yard trees are $2 to $6. At $4 to $6 per tree per year, administrative costs are significant for public trees. Removal and disposal expenditures, annualized over 40 years, average $2 to $3 per tree.

Table 3 shows annual management costs 20 years after planting for yard trees to the west of a house and for public trees. Annual costs for yard trees range from $3 to $8, and public tree care costs are $11 to $18. In general, public trees are more expensive to maintain than yard trees because of their prominence and because of the greater need for public safety.

Average Annual Benefits

Average annual benefits, including stormwater reduction, aesthetic value, air quality improvement, and carbon dioxide (CO_2) sequestration increase with mature tree size (figs. 17 and 18; for detailed results see app. 2):

- $15 to $21 for a small tree
- $27 to $35 for a medium tree
- $58 to $73 for a large tree

Stormwater runoff reduction—
By intercepting rain and snow before it reaches the stormwater treatment system, trees can reduce runoff. Of the environmental benefits provided by trees in the Lower Midwest, stormwater runoff reduction benefits are the greatest. The hackberry intercepts 4,808 gal per year on average over a 40-year period with an implied value of $30. The eastern redbud and littleleaf linden intercept 1,116, and 1,870 gal per year on average, with values of $7 and $12, respectively. Forty years

Table 3—Estimated annual costs 20 years after planting for a private tree opposite the west-facing wall and a public tree

Costs	Eastern redbud small tree 20 ft tall 20-ft spread LSA = 1,056 ft²		Littleleaf linden medium tree 29 ft tall 24-ft spread LSA = 1,414 ft²		Northern hackberry large tree 51 ft tall 36-ft spread LSA = 4,718 ft²	
	Private west	Public tree	Private west	Public tree	Private west	Public tree
	Dollars per tree per year					
Pruning	0.52	2.99	4.20	5.60	4.20	5.60
Remove and dispose	1.95	1.77	2.67	2.43	2.88	2.62
Pest and disease	0.09	0.11	0.12	0.15	0.13	0.16
Infrastructure	0.17	1.19	0.24	1.63	0.26	1.75
Cleanup	0.12	0.82	0.16	1.12	0.18	1.21
Liability and legal	0.01	0.04	0.01	0.05	0.01	0.06
Admin. and other	0.00	4.26	0.00	5.85	0.00	6.30
Total costs	2.86	11.17	7.40	16.82	7.65	17.71
Total benefits	21.48	21.23	36.61	35.06	77.43	74.55
Total net benefits	18.63	10.06	29.22	18.23	69.78	56.85

Note: Prices for removal and disposal are included to account for expected mortality of citywide planting.

LSA = leaf surface area.

after planting, stormwater runoff reductions equal 1,814, 3,526, and 8,382 gal for the small, medium, and large deciduous trees, respectively.

As the cities of the Lower Midwest continue to grow, the amount of impervious surface will continue to increase dramatically. The role that trees, in combination with other strategies such as rain gardens and structural soils, can play in reducing stormwater runoff is substantial.

Energy savings are substantial

Energy savings—

Energy benefits are the next largest environmental benefit and tend to increase with mature tree size. For example, average annual net energy benefits over the 40-year period are $4 for the small eastern redbud tree opposite a west-facing wall, $8 for the littleleaf linden, and $15 for the larger hackberry. For species of all sizes, energy savings increase as trees mature and their leaf surface area increases (figs. 17 and 18).

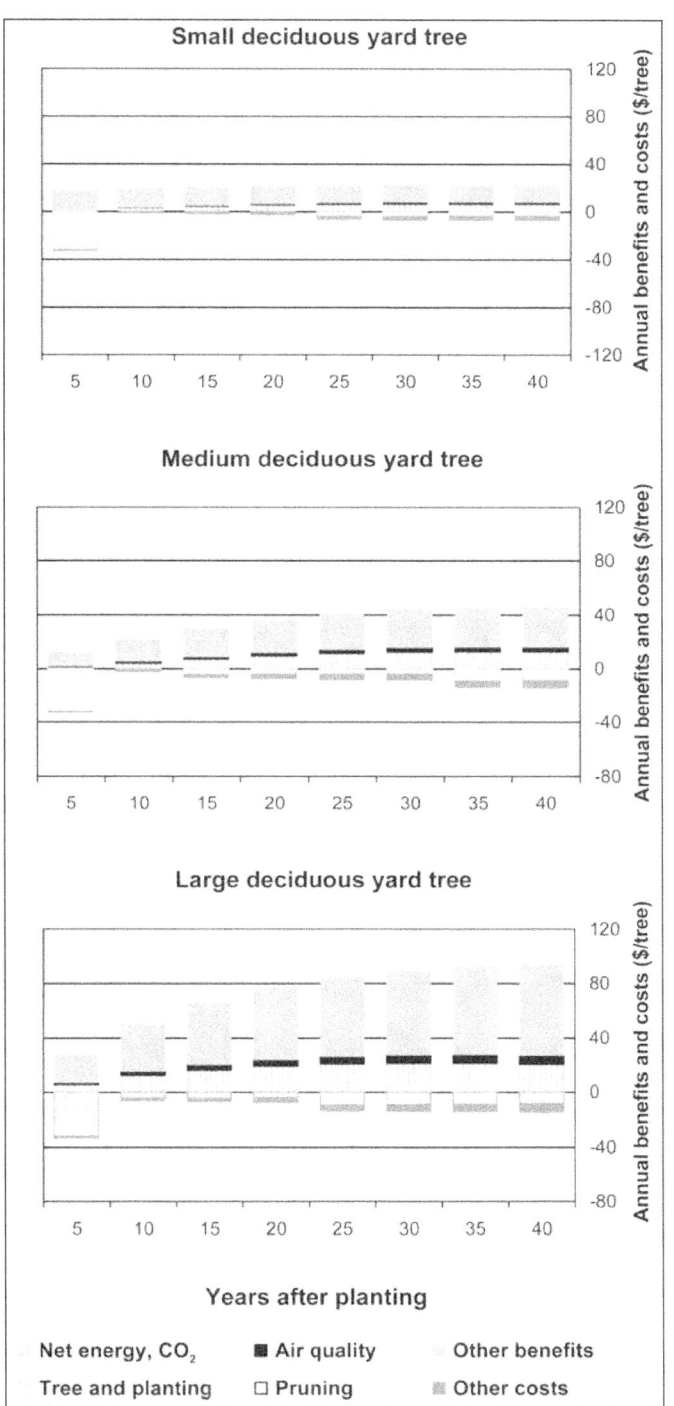

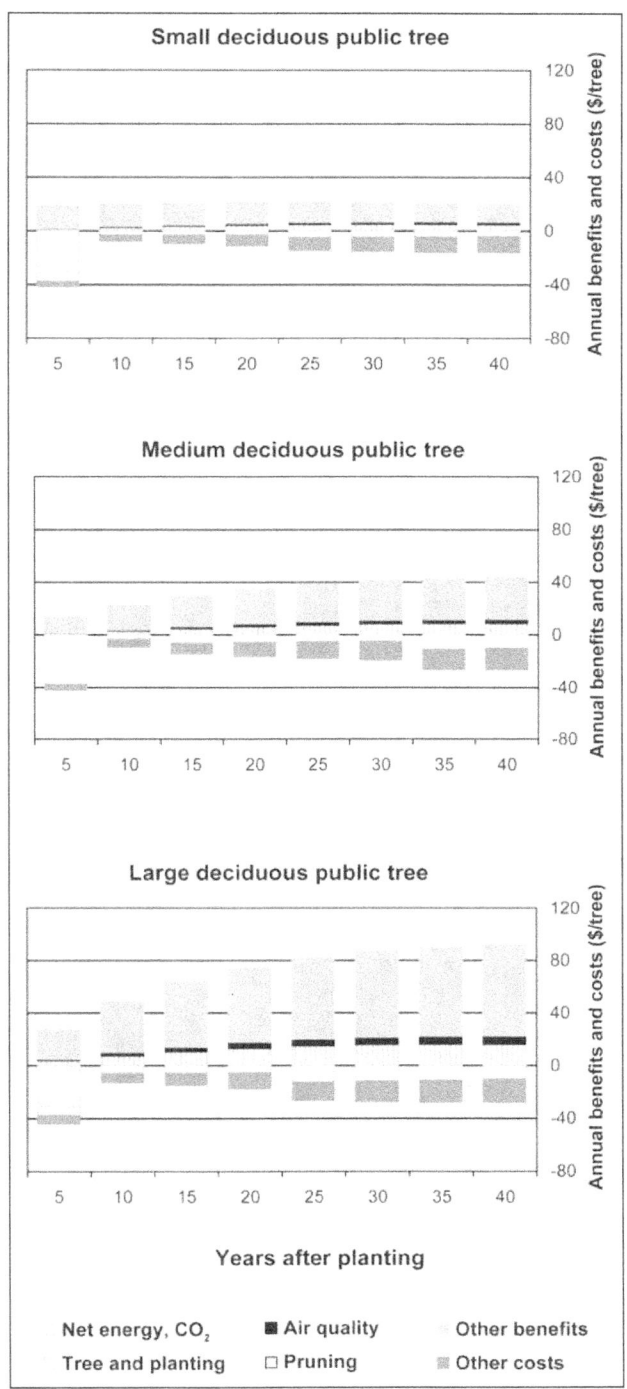

Figure 17— Estimated annual benefits and costs for a small (eastern redbud), medium (littleleaf linden), and large (northern hackberry) deciduous tree located west of a residence. Costs are greatest during the initial establishment period, whereas benefits increase with tree size.

Figure 18—Estimated annual benefits and costs per tree for public small (eastern redbud), medium (littleleaf linden), and large (northern hackberry) deciduous tree.

As might be expected in a region with hot, humid summers, cooling savings are substantial. Trees planted on the west side of buildings have the greatest total energy benefits because the effect of shade on cooling costs is maximized without blocking the warming rays of the winter sun. A yard tree located south of a home produced the least total energy benefit because it had the least benefit during the summer and the greatest adverse effect from shade on heating costs in winter. Trees located east of a building provided intermediate benefits. Total energy benefits also reflect species-related traits such as size, form, branch pattern, and density, as well as time in leaf.

Average annual total energy benefits for public trees were less than for yard trees and ranged from $3, $5, and $11 for the redbud, linden, and hackberry, respectively.

Air Quality Improvement—

Air quality benefits are defined as the sum of pollutant uptake by trees and avoided powerplant emissions from energy savings minus biogenic volatile organic compounds (BVOCs) released by trees. Average annual air quality benefits for the 40-year period are $1 for the redbud, $2 for the linden, and $4 for the hackberry. These relatively low air quality benefits reflect the clean air in the Lower Midwest region, where cities previously listed by the U.S. EPA for being in violation of federal air quality standards are now considered maintenance areas and no longer in violation. Contrast these results with the air quality benefits of a large tree in the Northeast region ($13; McPherson et al. 2007), Midwest region ($7.65; McPherson et al. 2006c), and southern California ($28.38; McPherson 2000) where air quality is poorer.

Reduced sulfur dioxide emissions due to trees reducing energy use produce the greatest air quality benefit. Over 40 years, the hackberry, for example, is estimated to reduce an average of 1.86 lb of sulfur dioxide from the air annually, valued at $2.79. Average annual reductions in ozone, **nitrogen oxides**, and particulate matter (PM_{10}) for the large tree are valued at $0.56, $0.47, and $0.44, respectively. Of the three species, only the linden is an emitter of BVOCs (0.21 lb per year), but the 40-year average cost of these emissions are nearly negligible at $-0.06 per tree.

Forty years after planting, the average annual monetary values of air quality improvement for the redbud, linden, and hackberry are $2, $3, and $5, respectively.

Carbon dioxide reduction—

Net atmospheric CO_2 reductions accrue for all tree types. Average annual net reductions range from a high of 591 lbs ($1.97) for a large public tree to a low of 37 lbs ($0.12) for a small tree on the southern side of the house. Deciduous trees opposite west-facing house walls generally produce the greatest CO_2 reduction because of reduced powerplant emissions associated with energy savings. The values for the redbud tree are lowest for CO_2 reduction reflecting this small tree's minor effect on energy savings and sequestration.

Forty years after planting, net CO_2 benefits for a yard tree opposite a west wall are 203, 389, and 715 lb for the small, medium, and large deciduous tree, respectively. Releases of CO_2 associated with tree care activities account for less than 1 percent of net CO_2 sequestration.

Aesthetic and other benefits—

Aesthetic and other benefits reflected in property values account for a significant portion of total benefits. As trees grow and become more visible, they can increase a property's sales price. Annual values averaged over 40 years associated with these aesthetic and other benefits for yard trees are $8, $12, and $22 for the small, medium, and large deciduous trees, respectively. The values for public trees are $8, $14, and $24, respectively. The values for yard trees are slightly less than for public trees because offstreet trees contribute less to a property's curb appeal than more prominent street trees. Because our estimates are based on median home sales prices, the effects of trees on property values and aesthetics will differ depending on local economies.

Chapter 4. Estimating Benefits and Costs for Tree Planting Projects in Your Community

This chapter shows two ways that benefit-cost information presented in this guide can be used. The first hypothetical example demonstrates how to adjust values from the guide for local conditions when the goal is to estimate benefits and costs for a proposed tree planting project. The second example explains how to compare net benefits derived from planting different types of trees. The last section discusses actions communities can take to increase the cost-effectiveness of their tree programs.

Applying Benefit-Cost Data

Flint Falls Example

The hypothetical city of Flint Falls is located in the Lower Midwest region and has a population of 24,000. Most of its street trees were planted decades ago, with English elms and silver maples (see "Common and Scientific Names" section) as the dominant species. Currently, the **tree canopy cover** is sparse because a number of trees died after drought conditions made them more susceptible to pests, and they have not been replaced. Many of the remaining street trees are in declining health. The city hired an urban forester 2 years ago and an active citizens group, the Green Team, has formed (fig. 19).

Initial discussions among the Green Team, local utilities, the urban forester, and other partners led to a proposed urban forestry program. The program intends to plant 1,000 trees in Flint Falls over a 5-year period. Trained volunteers will plant 3-in diameter trees in the following proportions: 75 percent large-maturing trees, 20 percent medium-maturing trees, and 5 percent small-maturing trees. One hundred trees will be planted in parks, and the remaining 900 trees will be planted along Main Street and other downtown streets. Mortality rates for earlier planting projects have been high, so the Green Team and the urban forester will concentrate their planting efforts in areas that are likely to be most successful, including planting spaces with sufficient soil capacity for trees to grow and as little conflict with infrastructure as possible, and that maximize environmental benefits. They expect to find a number of good suggestions for planting in chapter 5 of this guide.

The Flint Falls City Council has agreed to maintain the current funding level for management of existing trees. Also, they will advocate formation of a municipal tree district to raise funds for the proposed tree-planting project. A municipal tree district is similar in concept to a landscape assessment district, which receives

Figure 19—The (hypothetical) Green Team is motivated to re-green their community by planting 1,000 trees in 5 years.

revenues based on formulas that account for the services different customers receive. For example, the proximity of customers to greenspace in a landscape assessment district may determine how much they pay for upkeep. A municipal tree district might receive funding from air quality districts, stormwater management agencies, electric utilities, businesses, and residents in proportion to the value of future benefits these groups will receive from trees in terms of air quality, hydrology, energy, carbon dioxide (CO_2), and property value. The formation of such a district would require voter approval of a special assessment that charges recipients for tree planting and maintenance costs in proportion to the benefits they receive from the new trees. The council needs to know the amount of funding required for tree planting and maintenance, as well as how the benefits will be distributed over the 40-year life of the project.

As a first step, the Flint Falls city forester and Green Team decided to use the tables in appendix 2 to quantify total cumulative benefits and costs over 40 years for the proposed planting of 1,000 public trees—750 large, 200 medium, and 50 small deciduous.

Before setting up a spreadsheet to calculate benefits and costs, the team considered which aspects of Flint Falls' urban and community forestry project differ from the regional values used in this guide (the methods for calculating the values in app. 2 are described in app. 3):

1. The prices of electricity and natural gas in Flint Falls are $0.075 per kWh and $1.15 per therm, not $0.068 per kWh and $0.973 per therm as used in this guide. It is assumed that the buildings that will be shaded by the new street trees have air conditioning and natural-gas heating.

2. The Green Team projected future annual costs for monitoring tree health and implementing their stewardship program. Administration costs are estimated to average $2,500 annually for the life of the trees or $2.50 per tree each year. This guide assumed an average annual administration cost of $3.88 per tree. Thus, an adjustment is necessary.

3. Planting will cost $200 per tree. The guide assumes planting costs of $155 per tree. The costs will be higher for Flint Falls because they have decided to plant larger trees.

To calculate the dollar value of total benefits and costs for the 40-year period, the forester created a spreadsheet table (table 4). Each benefit and cost category is listed in the first column. Prices, adjusted where necessary for Flint Falls, are entered into the second column. The third column contains the **resource units** (RUs) per tree per year associated with the benefit or the cost per tree per year, which can be found in appendix 2. For aesthetic and other benefits, the dollar values for public trees are placed in the RU columns. The fourth column lists the 40-year total values, obtained by multiplying the RU values by tree numbers, prices, and 40 years.

To adjust for higher electricity prices, the forester multiplied electricity saved for a large public tree in the RU column (98 kWh) by the Flint Falls price for electricity ($0.075/kWh). This value ($7.35 per tree per year) was multiplied by the number of trees planted and 40 years ($7.35 × 750 trees × 40 years = $220,500) to obtain cumulative air-conditioning energy savings for the large public trees (table 4). The process was carried out for all benefits and all tree types.

First step: determine tree planting numbers

Second step: adjust for local prices of benefits

Third step: adjust for local costs

Fourth step: calculate net benefits and benefits-cost ratios for public trees

Table 4—Spreadsheet calculations of benefits and costs for the Flint Falls planting project (1,000 trees) over 40 years

Benefits	Adjusted price	50 small trees		200 medium trees		750 large trees		1,000 total trees		
	Dollars	Resource units	Total value	Resource units	Total value	Resource units	Total value	Total value		Percentage of benefits
		RU/tree/yr	Dollars	RU/tree/yr	Dollars	RU/tree/yr	Dollars	Dollars	$/tree/yr	
Electricity (kWh)	0.0750	29	4,350	45	27,000	98	220,500	251,850	6.30	10.2
Natural gas (therms)	1.15	1	2,300	2	18,400	4	138,000	158,700	3.97	6.5
Net carbon dioxide (lb)	0.00334	91	608	150	4,008	374	37,475	42,091	1.05	1.7
Ozone (lb)	0.825	0.20	330	0.32	2,112	0.68	16,829	19,271	0.48	—
Nitrogen dioxide (lb)	0.825	0.16	264	0.27	1,782	0.57	14,106	16,152	0.40	—
Sulfur dioxide (lb)	1.50	0.53	1,590	0.89	10,677	1.86	83,676	95,943	2.40	—
Small particulate matter (lb)	0.99	0.15	297	0.27	2,141	0.45	13,384	15,823	0.40	6.0
Volatile organic compounds (lb)	0.30	0.04	24	0.07	170	0.15	1,367	1,561	0.04	—
Biogenic volatile organic compounds (lb)	0.30	0.00	0	-0.21	-510	0.00	0	-510	-0.01	—
Hydrology (gal)	0.0062	1,116	13,838	1,870	92,752	4,808	894,288	1,000,878	25.02	40.7
Aesthetics and other		8.48	16,960	13.81	110,480	29.32	728,400	855,840	21.40	34.8
Total benefits			40,562		269,012		2,148,026	2,457,599	61.44	100.0
Costs			Total $		Total $		Total $	Total $	$/tree/yr	Percentage of costs
		$/tree/yr		$/tree/yr		$/tree/yr				
Tree and planting		5.00	10,000	5.00	40,000	5.00	150,000	200,000	5.00	24.3
Pruning		4.54	9,077	6.26	50,057	8.47	254,064	313,198	7.83	38.1
Remove and dispose		1.74	3,471	2.39	19,121	2.64	79,177	101,769	2.54	12.4
Infrastructure repair		1.08	2,153	1.47	11,793	1.61	48,267	62,213	1.56	7.6
Cleanup		0.74	1,487	1.02	8,144	1.11	33,332	42,964	1.07	5.2
Liability and legal		0.03	68	0.05	370	0.05	1,515	1,953	0.05	0.2
Admin. and other		2.50	5,000	2.50	20,000	2.50	75,000	100,000	2.50	12.2
Total costs			31,256		149,485		641,356	822,097	20.55	100.0
Net benefit			9,306		119,526		1,506,670	1,635,502	40.89	
Benefit/cost ratio			1.30		1.80		3.35	2.99		

RU = resource unit.

To adjust cost figures, the city forester changed the planting cost from $155 assumed in the guide to $200 (table 4). This planting cost was annualized by dividing the cost per tree by 40 years ($200/40 = $5.00 per tree per year). Total planting costs were calculated by multiplying this value by 750 large trees and 40 years ($150,000).

The administration, inspection, and outreach costs are expected to average $2.50 per tree per year. Consequently, the total administration cost for large trees is $2.50 × 750 large trees × 40 years ($75,000). The same procedure was followed to calculate costs for the medium and small trees.

All costs and all benefits were summed. Annual benefits over 40 years for the whole planting total $2.46 million ($61.44 per tree per year), and annual costs total about $822,000 ($20.55 per tree per year). Subtracting total costs from total benefits yields net benefits over the 40-year period:

- $9,306 or $4.65 per tree per year for small deciduous trees
- $119,526 or $14.94 per tree per year for medium deciduous trees
- $1,506,670 or $50.22 per tree per year for large deciduous trees

Dividing total benefits by total costs yielded benefit-cost ratios (BCRs) of 1.30, 1.80, and 3.35 for small, medium, and large deciduous trees, respectively. The BCR for the entire planting is 2.99, indicating that $2.99 will be returned for every $1 invested.

This analysis assumes 43 percent of the planted trees die and does not account for the time value of money from a capital investment perspective. Use the municipal discount rate to compare this investment in tree planting and management with alternative municipal investments.

Final step: determine how benefits are distributed, and link these to sources of revenues

The city forester and Green Team now know that the project will cost about $822,000, and the average annual cost will be $20,550 ($822,000/40 years); however, a higher proportion of funds will be needed initially for planting and irrigation. The fifth and last step is to identify the distribution of functional benefits that the trees will provide. The last column in table 4 shows the distribution of benefits as a percentage of the total:

- Energy savings = 16 percent (cooling = 10 percent, heating = 6 percent)
- CO_2 reduction = 2 percent
- Air quality improvement = 6 percent
- Stormwater runoff reduction = 41 percent
- Aesthetics/property value increase = 35 percent

Distributing costs of tree management to multiple parties

With this information the planning team can determine how to distribute the costs for tree planting and maintenance based on who benefits from the services the trees will provide. For example, assuming the goal is to generate enough annual revenue to cover the total costs of managing the trees ($822,000), fees could be distributed in the following manner:

- $131,520 from electric and natural gas utilities for peak energy savings (16 percent). (Utility companies invest in planting trees because it is more cost effective to reduce peak energy demand than to meet peak needs through added infrastructure.)
- $16,440 from local industry for atmospheric CO_2 reductions (2 percent).
- $49,320 from air quality management district for net reduction in air pollutants (6 percent).
- $337,020 from the stormwater management district for water quality improvement associated with reduced runoff (41 percent).
- $287,700 from property owners for increased property values (35 percent).

Whether funds are sought from partners, the general fund, or other sources, this information can assist managers in developing policy, setting priorities, and making decisions. The Center for Urban Forest Research has developed a computer program called STRATUM that simplifies these calculations for analysis of existing street tree populations (Maco and McPherson 2003; for more information, see www.itreetools.org; USDA FS 2006a).

City of Sandy Creek Example

Ten years ago, as a cost-cutting measure, the hypothetical city of Sandy Creek stopped planting street trees in areas of new development. Instead, developers were required to plant front yard trees, thereby reducing costs to the city. The community forester and concerned citizens came to notice that instead of the large, stately trees the city had once planted, developers were planting small flowering trees, which were more aesthetically pleasing in early years, but would never achieve the stature—or the benefits—of larger shade trees. To evaluate the consequences of these changes, the community forester and citizens decided to compare the benefits of planting small, medium, and large trees for a hypothetical street-tree planting project in a new neighborhood in Sandy Creek.

First step: calculate benefits and costs over 40 years

As a first step, the city forester and concerned citizens decided to quantify the total cumulative benefits and costs over 40 years for three potential street tree planting scenarios in Sandy Creek. The scenarios compare plantings of 500 small trees, 500 medium trees, and 500 large trees. Data in appendix 2 are used for the calculations; however, three aspects of Sandy Creek's urban and community forestry program are different from those assumed in this tree guide:

1. The price of electricity is $0.075/kWh, not $0.068/kWh.
2. The city will provide irrigation for the first 5 years at a cost of approximately $0.50 per tree annually.
3. Planting costs are $225 per tree for trees instead of $155 per tree.

To calculate the dollar value of total benefits and costs for the 40-year period, the last column in the appendix 2 tables (40-year average) is multiplied by 40 years. Because this value is for one tree, it must be multiplied by the total number of trees planted in the respective small, medium, or large tree size classes. To adjust for higher electricity prices, we multiply electricity saved per tree in the resource unit (RU) column (tables 6, 9, 12, and 15) for each tree type by the number of trees and 40 years (large tree: 98 kWh × 500 trees × 40 years = 1,960,000 kWh). This value is multiplied by the price of electricity in Sandy Creek ($0.075/kWh × 1,960,000 kWh = $147,000) to obtain cumulative air-conditioning energy savings for the project (table 5).

All the benefits are summed for each size tree for a 40-year period. The 500 small trees provide $382,611 in total benefits. The medium and large trees provide approximately $627,000 and $1.3 million, respectively.

To adjust cost figures, we add a value for irrigation by multiplying the annual cost by the number of trees and by the number of years that irrigation will be applied ($0.50 × 500 trees × 5 years = $1,250). We multiply 500 large trees by the unit planting cost ($225) to obtain the adjusted cost for planting (500 × $225 = $112,500). The average annual 40-year costs taken from appendix 2 for other items are multiplied by 40 years and the number of trees to compute total costs. These 40-year cost values are entered into table 5. The total costs for the small, medium and large trees are $353,850, $443,650, and $507,050.

Subtracting total costs from total benefits yields net benefits for the small ($28,761), medium ($183,405), and large ($833,846) trees (table 5). The net benefits per street tree over the 40-year period are as follows:

- $58 for a small tree
- $367 for a medium tree
- $1,668 for a large tree

When small trees are planted instead of large trees, the residents of Sandy Creek stand to lose more than $1,600 per tree. In a new neighborhood with 500 trees, the total loss of benefits would exceed $800,000 over the project lifetime.

Second step: adjust for local prices of benefits

Third step: adjust for local costs

Fourth step: calculate cost savings and benefits forgone

Table 5—Spreadsheet calculations of benefits and costs for the Sandy Creek planting project comparison over 40 years

	500 small		500 medium		500 large	
	Resource unit	Total value	Resource unit	Total value	Resource unit	Total value
		Dollars		*Dollars*		*Dollars*
Benefits:						
Electricity (kWh)	580,000	43,500	900,000	67,500	1,960,000	147,000
Natural gas (therms)	20,000	230	40,000	460	80,000	920
Net carbon dioxide (lb)	1,820,000	6,067	3,000,000	9,991	7,480,000	24,959
Ozone (lb)	3,930	3,244	6,340	5,231	13,580	11,206
Nitrogen dioxide (lb)	3,150	2,600	5,450	4,498	11,380	9,388
Sulfur dioxide (lb)	10,530	15,791	17,830	26,734	37,230	55,824
Small particulate matter (lb)	2,960	2,934	5,480	5,436	8,980	8,899
Volatile organic compounds (lb)	820	249	1,400	426	2,920	888
Biogenic volatile organic compounds (lb)	0	0	-4,230	-1,286	0	0
Hydrology (gal)	22,320,000	138,334	37,400,000	231,800	96,160,000	596,199
Aesthetics and other benefits		169,661		276,264		485,613
Total benefits		382,611		627,055		1,340,896
Costs:						
Tree and planting		112,500		112,500		112,500
Pruning		90,800		125,200		169,400
Remove and dispose		34,800		47,800		52,800
Infrastructure		21,600		29,400		32,200
Irrigation		1,250		1,250		1,250
Cleanup		14,800		20,400		22,200
Liability and legal		600		1,000		1,000
Admin. and other		77,400		106,000		115,600
Total costs		353,850		443,650		507,050
Net benefits		28,761		183,405		833,846
Benefit-cost ratio		1.08		1.41		2.64

Based on this analysis, the city of Sandy Creek decided to develop and enforce a street tree ordinance that requires planting large trees where possible and requires tree shade plans that show how developers will achieve 50 percent shade over streets, sidewalks, and parking lots within 15 years of development (fig. 20).

This analysis assumes that 43 percent of the planted trees died. It does not account for the time value of money from a capital investment perspective, but this could be done by using the municipal discount rate.

Pam Louks

Figure 20—A policy such as Sandy Creek's, to plant as large a tree as the site will handle, has provided ample benefits in the past. Here, large-growing trees have been planted.

Increasing Program Cost-Effectiveness

What if the program you have designed looks promising in terms of stormwater-runoff reduction, energy savings, volunteer participation, and additional benefits, but the costs are too high? This section describes some steps to consider that may increase benefits and reduce costs, thereby increasing cost-effectiveness.

Increasing Benefits

Improved stewardship to increase the health and survival of recently planted trees is one strategy for increasing cost-effectiveness. An evaluation of the Sacramento Shade program found that tree survival rates had a substantial impact on projected benefits (Hildebrandt et al. 1996). Higher survival rates increase energy savings and reduce tree removal and planting costs.

What if costs are too high?

Work to increase survival rates

Target tree planting with highest return

Customize planting locations

Reduce up-front and establishment costs

Prune early

Conifers and broadleaf evergreens intercept rainfall and particulate matter year round as well as reduce windspeeds and provide shade, which lowers summer cooling and winter heating costs. Locating these types of trees in yards, parks, school grounds, and other open-space areas can increase benefits.

Energy benefits can be further increased by planting a higher percentage of trees in locations that produce the greatest energy savings, such as opposite west-facing walls and close to buildings with air conditioning. Keep in mind that evergreen trees should not be planted on the southern side of buildings because their branches and leaves block the warm rays of the winter sun. By customizing tree locations to increase numbers in high-yield sites, energy savings can be boosted.

Reducing Program Costs

Cost effectiveness is influenced by program costs as well as benefits:

Cost effectiveness = total benefit / total program cost

Cutting costs is one strategy to increase cost effectiveness. A substantial percentage of total program cost occurs during the first 5 years and is associated with tree planting and establishment (McPherson 1993). Some strategies to reduce these costs include:

- Plant bare-root or smaller tree stock.
- Use trained volunteers for planting and pruning of young trees (fig. 21).
- Provide followup care to increase tree survival and reduce replacement costs.
- Select and locate trees to avoid conflicts with infrastructure.

Where growing conditions are likely to be favorable, such as yard or garden settings, it may be cost effective to use smaller, less expensive stock or bare-root trees. In highly urbanized settings and sites subject to vandalism, however, large stock may survive the initial establishment period better than small stock.

Although organizing and training volunteers requires labor and resources, it is usually less costly than contracting the work, and it can help build more support for your program. A cadre of trained volunteers can easily maintain trees until they reach a height of about 20 ft and limbs are too high to prune from the ground with pole pruners. By the time trees reach this size they are well established. Pruning during this establishment period should result in trees that will require less care in the long term. Training young trees can provide a strong branching structure that requires less frequent thinning and shaping (Costello 2000). Ideally, young trees should be inspected and pruned every other year for the first 5 years after planting.

Pam Louks

Figure 21—Trained volunteers can plant and maintain young trees, allowing the community to accomplish more at less cost and providing satisfaction for participants.

As trees grow larger, pruning costs may increase on a per-tree basis. The frequency of pruning will influence these costs, as it takes longer to prune a tree that has not been pruned in 10 years than one that was pruned a few years ago. Although pruning frequency differs by species and location, a return frequency of about 5 to 8 years is usually sufficient for older trees (Miller 1997).

Investing in the resources needed to promote tree establishment during the first 5 years after planting is usually worthwhile, because once trees are established they have a high probability of continued survival. If your program has targeted trees on private property, then encourage residents to attend tree-care workshops. Develop standards of "establishment success" for different types of tree species. Perform

Use less expensive stock where appropriate

Match tree to site

It all adds up—trees pay us back

periodic inspections to alert residents to tree health problems, and reward those whose trees meet your program's establishment standards. Replace dead trees as soon as possible, and identify ways to improve survivability.

Carefully select and locate trees to avoid conflicts with overhead power lines, sidewalks, and underground utilities. Time spent planning the planting will result in long-term savings. Also consider soil type and irrigation, microclimate, and the type of activities occurring around the tree that will influence its growth and management.

When evaluating the bottom line—trees pay us back—do not forget to consider benefits other than the stormwater-runoff reductions, energy savings, atmospheric CO_2 reductions, and other tangible benefits. The magnitude of benefits related to employment opportunities, job training, community building, reduced violence, and enhanced human health and well-being can be substantial (fig. 22). Moreover, these benefits extend beyond the site where trees are planted, furthering collaborative efforts to build better communities.

For more information on urban and community forestry program design and implementation, see the list of additional resources in appendix 1.

Brian Jorgenson

Figure 22—Trees pay us back in tangible and intangible ways.

Chapter 5. General Guidelines for Selecting and Placing Trees

Guidelines for Energy Savings
Maximizing Energy Savings From Shading

The right tree in the right place can save energy and reduce tree care costs. In midsummer, the sun shines on the east side of a building in the morning, passes over the roof near midday, and then shines on the west side in the afternoon (see fig. 4). Electricity use is highest during the afternoon when temperatures are warmest and incoming sunshine is greatest. Therefore, the west side of a home is the most important side to shade (Sand 1993) (fig. 23).

Depending on building orientation and window placement, sun shining through windows can heat a home quickly during the morning hours. The east side is the second most important side to shade when considering the net impact of tree shade on energy savings (fig. 23). Deciduous trees on the east side provide summer shade and more winter solar heat gain than evergreens.

Trees located to shade south walls can block winter sunshine and increase heating costs because during winter the sun is lower in the sky and shines on the south side of homes (fig. 24). The warmth the sun provides is an asset, and planting evergreen trees on the southern side of a home would block southern exposures and solar collectors. Use **solar-friendly trees** to the south because the bare branches of these deciduous trees allow most sunlight to strike the building (some solar-un-friendly deciduous trees can reduce sunlight striking the south side of buildings by

Where should shade trees be planted?

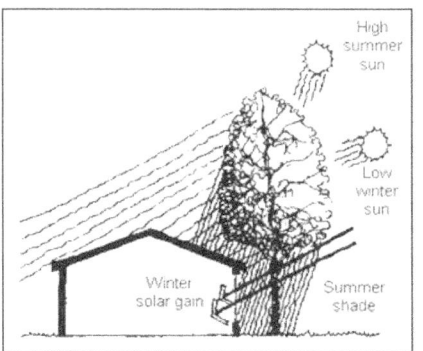

Figure 23—Locate trees to shade west and east windows (from Sand 1993).

Figure 24—Select solar-friendly trees for southern exposures and locate them close enough to provide winter solar access and summer shade (from Sand 1991).

50 percent even without leaves) (Ames 1987). Examples of solar-friendly trees include most species and **cultivars** of maples, crapemyrtle, honeylocust, sweetgum, and zelkova (see "Common and Scientific Names" section). Some solar-unfriendly trees include most oaks, sycamore, most elms, and river birch (McPherson et al. 1994).

To maximize summer shade and minimize winter shade, locate shade trees about 10 to 20 ft south of the home. As trees grow taller, prune lower branches to allow more sun to reach the building if this will not weaken the tree's structure (fig. 25).

Although the closer a tree is to a home the more shade it provides, roots of trees that are too close can damage the foundation. Branches too close to the building can make it difficult to maintain exterior walls and windows. Trees should be a minimum of 10 ft or farther from the home depending on mature crown spread, to avoid these conflicts. It should be noted, however, that trees within 30 to 50 ft of

Figure 25—Trees south of a home before and after pruning. Lower branches are pruned up to increase heat gain from winter sun (from Sand 1993).

the home most effectively shade windows and walls. Hence, larger growing trees may need pruning to avoid conflict with the structure and to systematically raise the crown until it has cleared the roofline.

Paved patios and driveways can become **heat sinks** that warm the home during the day. Shade trees can make them cooler and more comfortable spaces. If a home is equipped with an air conditioner, shading can reduce its energy use, but do not plant vegetation so close that it will obstruct the flow of air around the unit.

Plant only small-growing trees under overhead power lines, and avoid planting directly above underground water and sewer lines if possible. Contact your local utility company before planting to determine where underground lines are located and which tree species should not be planted below power lines.

Planting Windbreaks for Heating Savings

A tree's size and crown density can make it ideal for blocking wind, thereby reducing the impacts of cold winter weather. Locate rows of trees perpendicular to the prevailing wind (fig. 26), usually the north and west side of homes in the Lower Midwest region.

Design the windbreak row to be longer than the building being sheltered because windspeed increases at the edge of the windbreak. Ideally, the windbreak should be planted upwind about 25 to 50 ft from the building and should consist of dense evergreens that will grow to twice the height of the building they shelter (Heisler 1986, Sand 1991). Avoid planting windbreaks that will block sunlight to south and east walls (fig. 27). Trees should be spaced close enough to form a dense screen, but not so close that they will block sunlight to each other, causing lower

Plant dense ever-greens

Figure 26—Evergreens protect a building from dust and cold by reducing windspeeds (from Sand 1993).

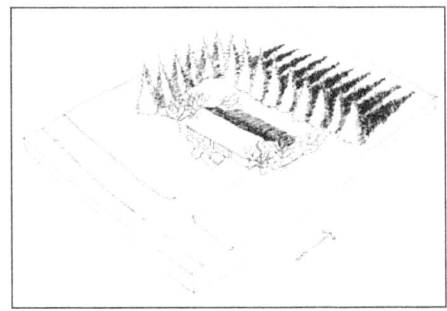

Figure 27—Midwinter shadows from a well-located windbreak and shade trees do not block solar radiation on the south-facing wall (from Sand 1993).

branches to self-prune. Most conifers can be spaced about 6 ft on center. If there is room for two or more rows, then space rows 10 to 12 ft apart.

Evergreens are preferred over deciduous trees for windbreaks because they provide better wind protection. The ideal windbreak tree is fast growing, visually dense, has strong branch attachments, and has stiff branches that do not self-prune. Your local cooperative extension agent or urban forester can help you select appropriate trees for your area.

In settings where vegetation is not a fire hazard, evergreens planted close to the home create airspaces that reduce air infiltration and heat loss. Allow shrubs to form thick hedges, especially along north, west, and east walls.

Selecting Trees to Maximize Benefits

There are many choices

The ideal shade tree has a fairly dense, round crown with limbs broad enough to partially shade the roof. Given the same placement, a large tree will provide more shade than a small tree. Deciduous trees allow sun to shine through leafless branches in winter. Plant small trees where nearby buildings or power lines limit aboveground space. Columnar trees are appropriate in narrow side yards. Because the best location for shade trees is relatively close to the west and east sides of buildings, the most suitable trees will be strong and capable of resisting storm damage, disease, and pests (Sand 1994). Examples of trees not to select for placement near buildings include cottonwoods and silver maples because of their invasive roots, weak wood, and large size, and ginkgos because of their sparse shade and slow growth during youth.

Picking the right tree

When selecting trees, match the tree's water requirements with those of surrounding plants. For instance, select low-water-use species for planting in areas that receive little irrigation. Also, match the tree's maintenance requirements with the amount of care and the type of use different areas in the landscape receive. For instance, tree species that drop fruit that can be a slip-and-fall problem should not be planted near paved areas that are frequently used by pedestrians. Check with your local landscape professional before selecting trees to make sure that they are well suited to the site's soil and climatic conditions.

Maximizing energy savings from trees

Use the following practices to plant and manage trees strategically to maximize energy conservation benefits:

- Increase community-wide tree canopy, and target shade to streets, parking lots, and other paved surfaces, as well as air-conditioned buildings.
- Shade west- and east-facing windows and walls.
- Select solar-friendly trees opposite east- and south-facing walls.

- Shade air conditioners, but don't obstruct airflow.
- Avoid planting trees too close to utilities and buildings.
- Where space permits, create multirow, evergreen windbreaks that are longer than the building.

Guidelines for Reducing Carbon Dioxide

Because trees in common areas and other public places may not shelter buildings from sun and wind and reduce energy use, carbon dioxide (CO_2) reductions are primarily due to sequestration. Fast-growing trees sequester more CO_2 initially than slow-growing trees, but this advantage can be lost if the fast-growing trees die at younger ages. Large trees have the capacity to store more CO_2 than smaller trees (fig. 28). To maximize CO_2 sequestration, select tree species that are well suited to the site where they will be planted. Consult with your local arborist to select the

Figure 28—Compared with small trees, large trees can store more carbon, filter more air pollutants, intercept more rainfall, and provide greater energy savings. Here maple trees line an Indianapolis street in Center Township.

right tree for your site. Trees that are not well adapted will grow slowly, show symptoms of stress, or die at an early age. Unhealthy trees do little to reduce atmospheric CO_2 and can be unsightly liabilities in the landscape.

Design and management guidelines that can increase CO_2 reductions include the following:

- Maximize use of woody plants, especially trees, as they store more CO_2 than do herbaceous plants and grasses.

- Plant more trees where feasible, and immediately replace dead trees to compensate for CO_2 lost through removal.

- Create diverse habitats, with trees of different ages and species, to promote a continuous canopy cover over time.

- Group species with similar landscape maintenance requirements together and consider how irrigation, pruning, fertilization, weed, pest, and disease control can be minimized.

- Reduce CO_2 associated with landscape management by using push mowers (not gas or electric), hand saws (not chain saws), pruners (not gas/electric shears), rakes (not leaf blowers), and employ landscape professionals who don't have to travel far to your site.

- Reduce maintenance by reducing turfgrass and planting drought-tolerant or environmentally friendly landscapes.

- Consider the project's lifespan when selecting species. Fast-growing species will sequester more CO_2 initially than slow-growing species, but may not live as long.

- Provide ample space belowground for tree roots to grow so that they can maximize CO_2 sequestration and tree longevity.

- When trees die or are removed, salvage as much wood as possible for use as furniture and other long-lasting products to delay decomposition.

- Plant trees, shrubs, and vines in strategic locations to maximize summer shade and reduce winter shade, thereby reducing atmospheric CO_2 emissions associated with power production.

Guidelines for Reducing Stormwater Runoff

Trees are minireservoirs, controlling runoff at the source because their leaves and branch surfaces intercept and store rainfall, thereby reducing runoff volumes and erosion of watercourses, as well as delaying the onset of peak flows. Rainfall interception by large trees is a relatively inexpensive first line of defense in the battle to control nonpoint-source pollution.

When selecting trees to maximize rainfall interception benefits, consider the following:

- Select tree species with physiological features that maximize interception, such as evergreen foliage, large leaf surface area, and rough surfaces that store water (Metro 2002).
- Increase interception by planting large trees where possible (fig. 29).
- Plant trees that are in leaf when precipitation levels are highest.
- Plant low-water-use tree species where appropriate and native species that, once established, require little supplemental irrigation.
- In bioretention areas, such as roadside swales, select species that tolerate inundation, are long-lived, wide-spreading, and fast-growing (Metro 2002).
- Do not pave over streetside planting strips for easier weed control; this can reduce tree health and increase runoff.
- Bioswales in parking lots and other paved areas store and filter stormwater while providing good conditions for trees.

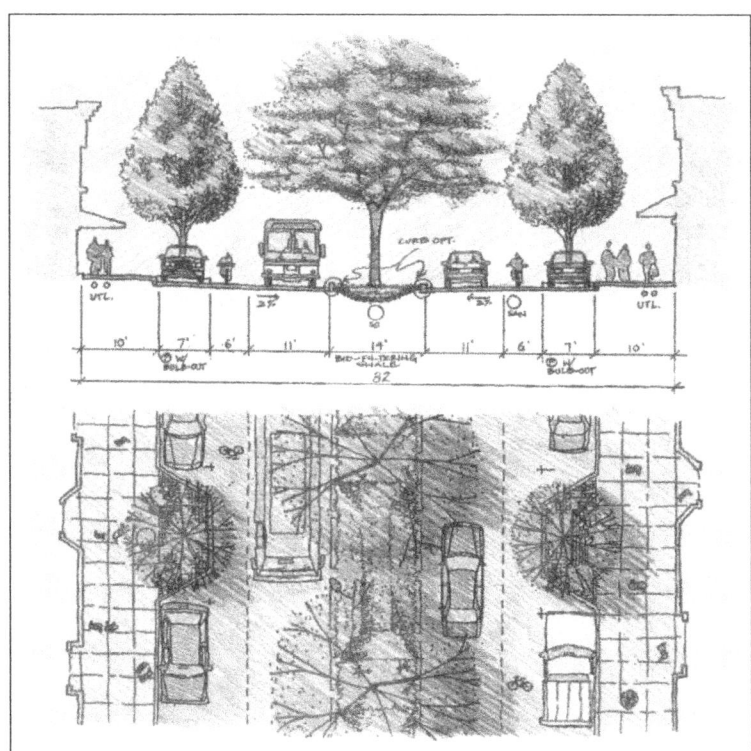

Figure 29—Trees can create a continuous canopy for maximum rainfall interception, even in commercial areas. In this example, a swale in the median filters runoff and provides ample space for large trees. Parking-space-sized planters contain the soil volume required to grow healthy, large trees (from Metro 2002).

Guidelines for Improving Air Quality Benefits

Trees, sometimes called the "lungs of our cities," are important because of their ability to remove contaminants from the air. The amount of gaseous pollutants and particulates removed by trees depends on their size and architecture, as well as local meteorology and pollutant concentrations.

Along streets, in parking lots, and in commercial areas, locate trees to maximize shade on paving and parked vehicles. Shade trees reduce heat that is stored or reflected by paved surfaces. By cooling streets and parking areas, trees reduce emissions of evaporative hydrocarbons from parked cars and thereby reduce smog formation (Scott et al. 1999). Large trees can shade a greater area than smaller trees, but should be used only where space permits. Remember that a tree needs space for both branches and roots. Keep in mind also that the soil along streets and parking lots will likely be compacted, and measures to reduce this problem, such as the use of engineered or structural soils, must be taken.

Tree planting and management guidelines to improve air quality include the following (Nowak 2000, Smith and Dochinger 1976):

- Select species that tolerate pollutants that are present in harmful concentrations. For example, in areas with high ozone (O_3) concentration, avoid sensitive species such as white and green ash, tulip, poplar, and Austrian pine (Noble et al. 1988).
- Conifers have high surface-to-volume ratios and retain their foliage year round, which may make them more effective than deciduous species. In parking areas, however, species should be carefully chosen to avoid those that give off sticky residues.
- Species with long leaf stems (e.g., ash, maple) and hairy plant parts (e.g., oak, birch, sumac) are especially efficient interceptors.
- Effective uptake depends on proximity to the pollutant source and the amount of biomass. Where space and fire conditions permit, plant multilayered stands near the source of pollutants.
- In areas with unhealthy O_3 concentrations, maximize use of plants that emit low levels of biogenic volatile organic compounds to reduce O_3 formation.
- Sustain large, healthy trees; they produce the most benefits.
- To reduce emissions of volatile organic compounds and other pollutants, plant trees to shade parked cars and conserve energy.

Guidelines for Avoiding Conflicts With Infrastructure

Trees can become liabilities when they conflict with power lines, underground utilities, and other infrastructure elements. Guidelines to reduce conflicts with infrastructure include the following:

- Before planting, contact your local before-digging company using the national 811 number to locate underground water, sewer, gas, and telecommunications lines.
- Avoid locating trees where they will block streetlights or views of traffic and commercial signs.
- Check with local transportation officials for sight visibility requirements. Keep trees at least 30 ft away from street intersections to ensure visibility.
- Avoid planting shallow-rooting species near sidewalks, curbs, and paving where tree roots can heave pavement if planted too close. Generally, avoid planting within 3 ft of pavement, and remember that trunk flare at the base of large trees can displace soil and paving for a considerable distance. Consider strategies to reduce damage by tree roots such as meandering sidewalks around trees (Costello and Jones 2003).
- Plant only small trees (<25 ft tall) under overhead power lines, and do not plant directly above underground water and sewer lines (fig. 30). Avoid locating trees where they will block illumination from streetlights or views of street signs in parking lots, commercial areas, and along streets.

Maintenance requirements and public safety concerns influence the type of trees selected for public places. The ideal public tree is not susceptible to wind damage and branch drop, does not require frequent pruning, produces negligible litter, is deep-rooted, has few serious pest and disease problems, and tolerates a wide range of soil conditions, irrigation regimes, and air pollutants. Because relatively few trees have all these traits, it is important to match the tree species to the planting site by determining what issues are most important on a case-by-case basis. For example, parking-lot trees should be tolerant of hot, dry conditions, have strong branch attachments, and be resistant to attacks by pests that leave vehicles covered with sticky exudates. Check with your local horticultural extension agency, state urban forestry program, or city forestry department for horticultural information on tree traits.

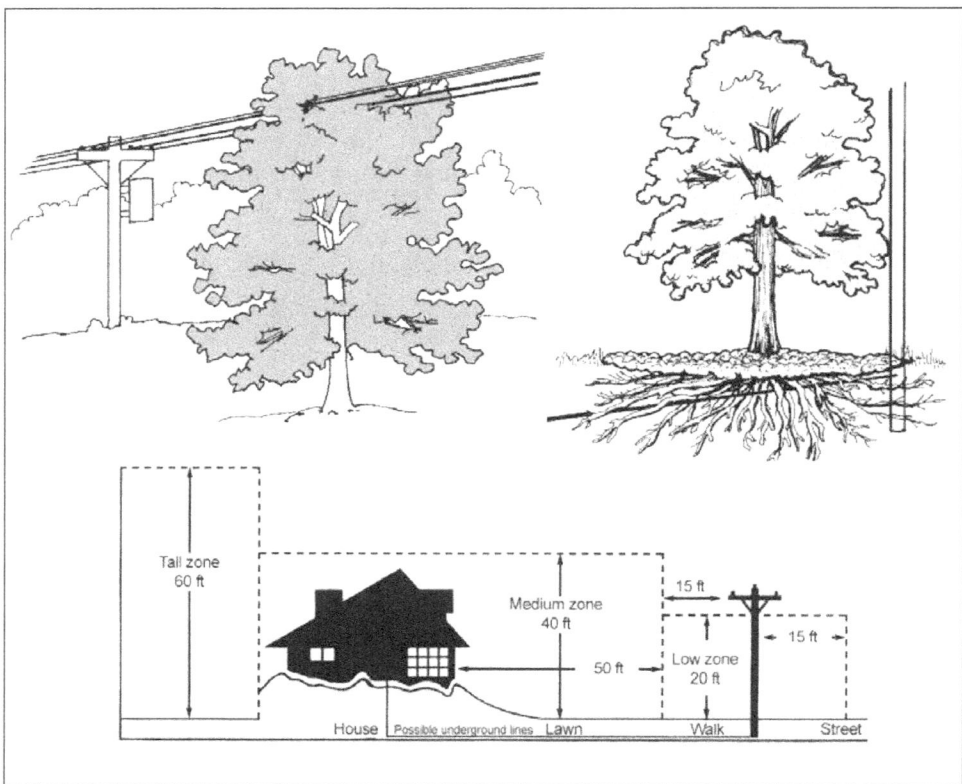

Figure 30—Know where power lines and other utility lines are before planting. Under power lines, use only small-growing trees ("low zone") and avoid planting directly above underground utilities. Larger trees may be planted where space permits ("medium" and "tall zones") (from ISA 1992).

Guidelines for Maximizing Long-Term Benefits

Selecting a tree from the nursery that has a high probability of becoming a healthy, trouble-free **mature tree** is critical to a successful outcome. Therefore, select the very best stock at your nursery and, when necessary, reject nursery stock that does not meet American National Standards Institute (ANSI) Z60-Nursery Stock standards.

The health of the tree's root ball is critical to its ultimate survival. If the tree is in a container, check for matted roots by sliding off the container. Roots should penetrate to the edge of the root ball, but not densely circle the inside of the container or grow through drain holes. As well, at least two large structural roots should emerge from the trunk within 1 to 3 in of the soil surface. If there are no roots in the upper portion of the root ball, it is undersized and the tree should not be planted.

Another way to evaluate the quality of the tree before planting is to gently move the trunk back and forth. A good tree trunk bends and does not move in the soil, whereas a poor trunk bends a little and pivots at or below the soil line—a tell-tale sign of a poorly anchored tree.

Dig the planting hole 1 in shallower than the depth of the root ball to allow for some settling after watering. Make the hole two to three times as wide as the root ball and loosen the sides of the hole to make it easier for roots to penetrate. Place the tree so that the root flare is at the top of the soil. If the structural roots have grown properly as described above, the top of the root ball will be slightly higher (1 to 2 in) than the surrounding soil to allow for settling. Backfill with the native soil unless it is very rocky or sandy, in which case you may want to add composted organic matter such as peat moss or shredded bark (fig. 31).

Planting trees in urban plazas, commercial areas, and parking lots poses special challenges because of limited soil volume and poor soil structure. For trees to deliver benefits over the long term they require enough soil volume to grow and

A good tree is well-anchored

Plant the tree in the right size hole

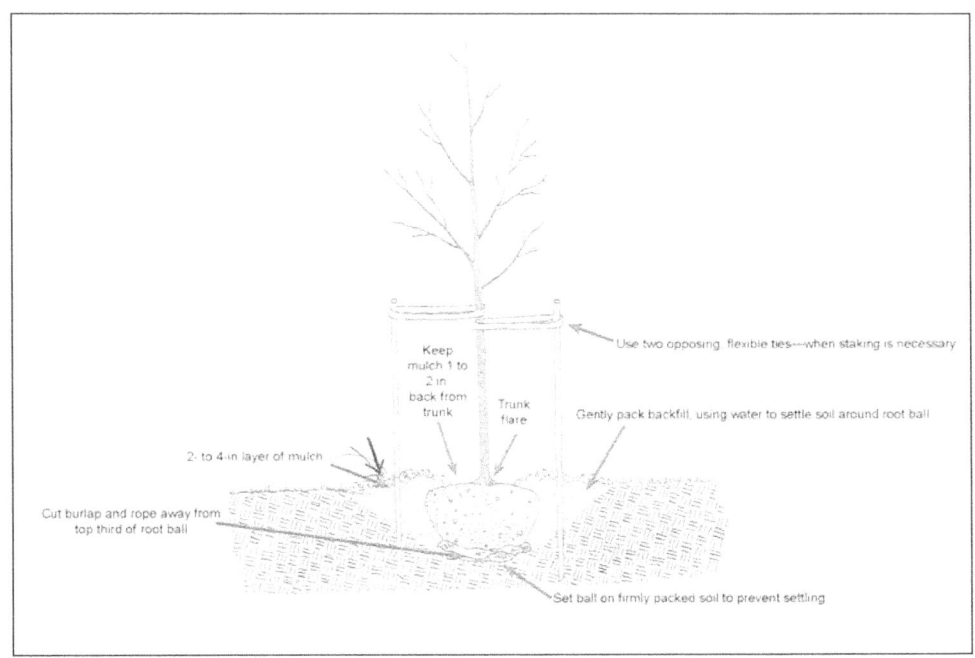

Figure 31— Prepare a broad planting area, plant the tree with the root flare at or just above ground level, and provide a berm/water ring to retain water (drawing courtesy of International Society of Arboriculture). (Note that trunk flare shown here represents a tree grown under optimum conditions. In trees grown under poorer conditions, the trunk flare may be hidden beneath the soil. These trees should be rejected in favor of those grown more carefully, or at the very least, the soil should be removed to expose the flare. See American National Standards Institute (ANSI) A 300—Tree Planting Standards).

remain healthy. Matching tree species to the site's soil volume can reduce sidewalk and curb damage as well. Figure 32 shows recommended soil volumes for different-sized trees. Engineered or structural soils can be placed under the hardscape to increase rooting space while meeting engineering requirements. For more information on structural soils see *Reducing Infrastructure Damage by Tree Roots: A Compendium of Strategies* (Costello and Jones 2003).

Use the extra soil left after planting to build a berm outside the root ball that is 6 in high and 3 ft in diameter. Soak the tree, and gently rock it to settle it in. Cover the basin with a 2- to 4-in layer of mulch, but avoid placing mulch against the tree trunk. Water the new tree two to three times a week and increase the amount of water as the tree grows larger. Generally, a tree requires about 1 in of water per week. A rain gauge or soil moisture sensor (tensiometer) can help determine tree watering needs, or contact your local cooperative extension agent or water conservancy district for recommendations.

After you've planted your tree, remember the following:

- Inspect your tree several times a year, and contact a local landscape professional if problems develop.

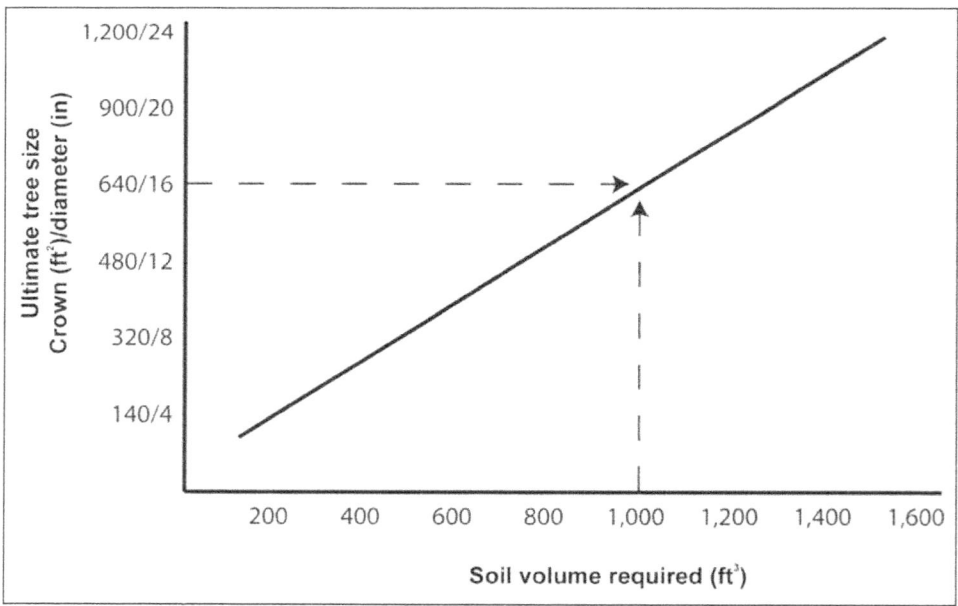

Figure 32—Developed from several sources by Urban (1992), this graph shows the relationship between tree size and required soil volume. For example, a tree with a 16-in diameter at breast height with 640 ft² of crown projection area requires 1,000 ft³ of soil (from Costello and Jones 2003).

- If your tree needed staking to keep it upright, remove the stake and ties after 1 year or as soon as the tree can hold itself up. The staking should allow some tree movement, as this movement sends hormones to the roots causing them to grow and create greater tree stability. It also promotes trunk taper and growth.

- Reapply mulch and irrigate the tree as needed.

- Leave lower side branches on young trees for the first year to increase taper. Remove dead, dying, and broken branches in the first year. Once established, prune young trees to maintain a central main trunk and equally spaced branches. For more information, see Costello (2000), Gilman (2002), and *ANSI A 300 Maintenance Standard Practices—Young Trees* 2008). As the trees mature, they should be pruned on a regular basis by a certified arborist or other experienced professional.

- By keeping your tree healthy, you maximize its ability to produce shade, intercept rainfall, reduce atmospheric CO_2, and provide other benefits.

For more information on tree selection, planting, establishment, and care, see the resources listed in appendix 1.

Glossary

annual fuel utilization efficiency (AFUE)—A measure of space heating equipment efficiency defined as the fraction of energy output per energy input.

anthropogenic—Produced by humans.

biodiversity—The variety of life forms in a given area. Diversity can be categorized in terms of the number of species, the variety in the area's plant and animal communities, the genetic variability of the animals or plants, or a combination of these elements.

biogenic—Produced by living organisms.

biogenic volatile organic compounds (BVOCs)—Hydrocarbon compounds from vegetation (e.g., isoprene, monoterpene) that exist in the ambient air and contribute to the formation of smog or may themselves be toxic. Emission rates ($\mu g \cdot g^{-1} \cdot hr^{-1}$) used for this report follow Benjamin and Winer (1998):

- *Celtis occidentalis*—0.0 (isoprene); 0.0 (monoterpene)

- *Tilia cordata*—1.6 (isoprene); 2.9 (monoterpene)

- *Cercis canadensis*—0.0 (isoprene); 0.0 (monoterpene)

canopy—A layer or multiple layers of branches and foliage at the top or crown of a forest's trees.

canopy cover—The area of land surface that is covered by tree canopy, as seen from above.

climate—The average weather for a particular region and period (usually 30 years). Weather describes the short-term state of the atmosphere; climate is the average pattern of weather for a particular region. Climatic elements include precipitation; temperature; humidity, sunshine; wind velocity; phenomena such as fog, frost, and hailstorms; and other measures of weather.

climate effects—Impact on residential space heating and cooling (kilograms of carbon dioxide per tree per year) from trees located more than 50 ft from a building owing to associated reductions in windspeeds and summer air temperatures.

community forests—The sum of all woody and associated vegetation in and around human settlements, ranging from small rural villages to metropolitan regions.

conifers—Cone-bearing evergreen trees with needle-like leaves.

contract rate—The percentage of residential trees cared for by commercial arborists; the proportion of trees for which a specific service (e.g., pruning or pest management) is contracted.

control costs—The marginal cost of preventing, controlling, or mitigating an impact.

crown—The branches and foliage at the top of a tree.

cultivar (derived from "cultivated variety")—Denotes certain cultivated plants that are clearly distinguishable from others by any characteristic, and that when reproduced (sexually or asexually), retain their distinguishing characteristics. In the United States, "variety" is often considered synonymous with "cultivar."

damage costs—The total estimated economic loss produced by an impact.

deciduous—Trees or shrubs that lose their leaves every fall.

diameter at breast height (d.b.h.)—The diameter of a tree outside the bark measured 4.5 ft above the ground on the uphill side (where applicable) of the tree.

dripline—The area beneath a tree marked by the outer edges of the branches.

emission factor—The rate of carbon dioxide, nitrogen dioxide, sulfur dioxide, and small particulate matter output resulting from the consumption of electricity, natural gas, or any other fuel source.

evapotranspiration—The total loss of water by evaporation from the soil surface and by transpiration from plants, from a given area, and during a specified period.

evergreens—Trees or shrubs that are never entirely leafless. Evergreens may be broadleaved or coniferous (cone-bearing with needlelike leaves).

greenspace—Urban trees, forests, and associated vegetation in and around human settlements, ranging from small communities in rural settings to metropolitan regions.

hardscape—Paving and other impervious ground surfaces that reduce infiltration of water into the soil.

heat sinks—Paving, buildings, and other surfaces that store heat energy from the sun.

hourly pollutant dry deposition—Removal of gases from the atmosphere by direct transfer to natural surfaces and absorption of gases and particles by natural surfaces such as vegetation, soil, water, or snow.

interception—Amount of rainfall held on tree leaves and stem surfaces.

kWh (kilowatt-hour)—A unit of work or energy, measured as 1 kW (1,000 watts) of power expended for 1 hour.

leaf area index (LAI)—Total leaf area per unit area of crown if crown were projected in two dimensions.

leaf surface area (LSA)—Measurement of area of one side of a leaf or leaves.

mature tree—A tree that has reached a desired size or age for its intended use. Size, age, and economic maturity differ depending on the species, location, growing conditions, and intended use.

mature tree size—The approximate size of a tree 40 years after planting.

metric tonne—A measure of weight (abbreviated "t") equal to 1,000,000 grams (1000 kg) or 2,205 pounds.

municipal forester—A person who manages public street or park trees (municipal forestry programs) for the benefit of the community.

MWh (megawatt-hour)—A unit of work or energy, measured as 1 megawatt (1,000,000 watts) of power expended for 1 hour. One MWh is equivalent to 3.412 MBtu.

nitrogen oxides (oxides of nitrogen, NO_x)—A general term for compounds of nitric acid (NO), nitrogen dioxide (NO_2), and other oxides of nitrogen. Nitrogen oxides are typically created during combustion processes and are major contributors to smog formation and acid deposition. NO_2 may cause numerous adverse human health effects.

ozone (O_3)—A strong-smelling, pale blue, reactive toxic chemical gas with molecules of three oxygen atoms. It is a product of the photochemical process involving the Sun's energy. Ozone exists in the upper layer of the atmosphere as well as at the Earth's surface. Ozone at the Earth's surface can cause numerous adverse human health effects. It is a major component of smog.

peak flow (or peak runoff)—The maximum rate of runoff at a given point or from a given area, during a specific period.

photosynthesis—The process in green plants of converting water and CO_2 into sugar by using light energy; accompanied by the production of oxygen.

PM_{10} (particulate matter)—Major class of air pollutants consisting of tiny solid or liquid particles of soot, dust, smoke, fumes, and mists. The size of the particles (10 microns or smaller, about 0.0004 in or less) allows them to enter the air sacs (gas-exchange region) deep in the lungs where they may be deposited and cause adverse health effects. PM_{10} also reduces visibility.

reduced powerplant emissions—Reduced emissions of carbon dioxide (CO_2) or other pollutants that result from reductions in building energy use owing to the moderating effect of trees on climate. Reduced energy use for heating and cooling results in reduced demand for electrical energy, which translates into fewer emissions by powerplants.

resource unit (RU)—The value used to determine and calculate benefits and costs of individual trees. For example, the amount of air conditioning energy saved in kWh/year per tree, air-pollutant uptake in pounds per year per tree, or rainfall intercepted in gallons per tree per year.

riparian habitats—Narrow strips of land bordering creeks, rivers, lakes, or other bodies of water.

seasonal energy efficiency ratio (SEER)—Ratio of cooling output to power consumption; kBtu-output/kWh-input as a fraction. It is the Btu of cooling output during normal annual usage divided by the total electric energy input in kilowatt-hours during the same period.

sequestration—Annual net rate that a tree removes CO_2 from the atmosphere through the processes of photosynthesis and respiration (kg of CO_2 per tree per year).

shade coefficient—The percentage of light striking a tree crown that is transmitted through gaps in the crown. This is the percentage of light that hits the ground.

shade effects—Impact on residential space heating and cooling (kg of CO_2 per tree per year) from trees located within 50 ft of a building.

solar-friendly trees—Trees that have characteristics that reduce blocking of winter sunlight. According to one numerical ranking system, these traits include open crowns during the winter heating season, leaves that fall early and appear late, relatively small size, and a slow growth rate (Ames 1987).

stem flow—Amount of rainfall that travels down the tree trunk and onto the ground.

sulfur dioxide (SO_2)—A strong-smelling, colorless gas that is formed by the combustion of fossil fuels. Powerplants, which may use coal or oil high in sulfur content, can be major sources of SO_2. Sulfur oxides contribute to the problem of acid deposition.

therm—A unit of heat equal to 100,000 British thermal units (BTUs) or 100 kBtu.

throughfall—Amount of rainfall that falls directly to the ground below the tree crown or drips onto the ground from branches and leaves.

transpiration—The loss of water vapor through the stomata of leaves.

tree or canopy cover—Within a specific area, the percentage covered by the crown of an individual tree or delimited by the vertical projection of its outermost perimeter; small openings in the crown are ignored. Used to express the relative importance of individual species within a vegetation community or to express the coverage of woody species.

tree litter—Fruit, leaves, twigs, and other debris shed by trees.

tree-related CO_2 emissions—CO_2 released when growing, planting, and caring for trees.

tree surface saturation storage capacity—The maximum volume of water that can be stored on a tree's leaves, stems, and bark. This part of rainfall stored on the canopy surface does not contribute to surface runoff during and after a rainfall event.

urban heat island—An area in a city where summertime air temperatures are 3 to 8 °F warmer than temperatures in the surrounding countryside. Urban areas are warmer for two reasons: (1) dark construction materials for roofs and asphalt absorb solar energy; and (2) few trees, shrubs, or other vegetation provide shade and cool the air.

volatile organic compounds (VOCs)—Hydrocarbon compounds that exist in the ambient air. VOCs contribute to the formation of smog or are themselves toxic. VOCs often have an odor. Some examples of VOCs are gasoline, alcohol, and the solvents used in paints.

willingness to pay—The maximum amount of money an individual would be willing to pay for nonmarket, public goods and services provided by environmental amenities such as trees and forests rather than do without.

Common and Scientific Names

Common name	Scientific name
Plants:	
American holly	*Ilex opaca* Aiton
Ash	*Fraxinus* spp.
Austrian pine	*Pinus nigra* J.F. Arnold
Birch	*Betula* spp.
Black oak	*Quercus velutina* Lam.
Blackgum	*Nyssa* spp.
Black walnut	*Juglans nigra* L.
Blue spruce	*Picea pungens* Engelm.
Callery pear	*Pyrus calleryana* Dcne.
Cottonwood	*Populus* spp.
Crabapple	*Malus* spp.
Crapemyrtle	*Lagerstroemia indica* L.
Eastern cottonwood	*Populus deltoides* Bartram ex Marsh.
Eastern redbud	*Cercis canadensis* L.
Eastern white pine	*Pinus strobus* L.
Elm	*Ulmus* spp.
English elm	*Ulmus procera* Salisb.
Ginkgo	*Ginkgo biloba* L.
Green ash	*Fraxinus pennsylvanica* Marsh.
Honeylocust	*Gleditsia triacanthos* L.
Littleleaf linden	*Tilia cordata* Mill.
Maple	*Acer* spp.
Mulberry	*Morus* spp.
Norway maple	*Acer platanoides* L.
Northern catalpa	*Catalpa speciosa* (Warder) Warder ex Engelm.
Northern hackberry	*Celtis occidentalis* L.
Northern red oak	*Quercus rubra* L.
Oak	*Quercus* spp.
Pear	*Pyrus* spp.
Poplar	*Populus* spp.
River birch	*Betula nigra* L.
Russian olive	*Elaeagnus angustifolia* L.
Siberian elm	*Ulmus pumila* L.
Silver maple	*Acer saccharinum* L.
Sugar maple	*Acer saccharum* Michx.
Sumac	*Rhus* spp.
Sweetgum	*Liquidambar styraciflua* L.
Sycamore	*Platanus* spp.
Tree-of-heaven	*Ailanthus altissima* (P. Mill.) Swingle
Tulip tree	*Liriodendron tulipifera* L.
White ash	*Fraxinus americana* L.
Zelkova	*Zelkova serrata* (Thunb.) Makino
Insects:	
Emerald ash borer	*Agrilus planipennis* Fairmaire

Metric Equivalents

When you know:	Multiply by:	To find:
Inches (in)	25,400	Microns
Inches (in)	25.4	Millimeters (mm)
Inches (in)	2.54	Centimeters (cm)
Feet (ft)	0.305	Meters (m)
Square feet (ft^2)	0.0929	Square meters (m^2)
Miles (mi)	1.61	Kilometers (km)
Square miles (mi^2)	2.59	Square kilometers (km^2)
Acre-feet	1233.6	Cubic meters (m^3)
Gallons (gal)	0.00378	Cubic meters (m^3)
Ounces	28.35	Grams (g)
Ounces	28,349,523	Micrograms (μg)
Pounds (lb)	0.454	Kilograms (kg)
Pounds per square foot (lb/ft^2)	4.882	Kilograms per square meter (kg/m^2)
Tons (ton)	0.907	Metric tonne (t)
Million BTUs	0.2931	Megawatt hours (MWh)
Therms	29.31	Kilowatt hours (kWh)
Fahrenheit (°F)	0.56 (F•32)	Celsius (°C)

Acknowledgments

A number of people assisted with data collection and provided technical assistance: Scott Maco, Jim Jenkins, and Aren Dottenwhy (Davey Resource Group); Lindsey Purcell, Paul Pinco, Perry Seitzinger, and Ashley Mulis (Forestry Section, Parks and Recreation Department, Indianapolis, Indiana); Jim Stout (Mapping and Geographic Infrastructure, Indianapolis, Indiana); Brian Brown (AMEC Earth & Environmental, Inc); Stephanie Huang, Christine Yang, Aywon-Anh Nguyen, and Linda George (Center for Urban Forest Research). A special thanks to Indiana Community Tree Stewards and members of the Indiana Urban Forest Council, Inc. for age-dating trees through ring counts.

Tree care expenditure information was provided by Lindsey Purcell and Paul Pinco (City of Indianapolis, Indiana), Scott Brewer (City of Carmel, Indiana), Paul Lindeman (City of Terre Haute, Indiana), Dave Gamstetter (City of Cincinnati, Ohio), Steven Spilatro (City of Marietta, Ohio), Scott Swain (Tree Care Specialists of Southern Ohio), David Kennedy (Kennedy's Arboriculture LLC), Eric Loveland and Aaron More (Brownsburg Tree Care), Felicia Clemons (Indiana Tree Service), and Jud Scott (Vine & Branch).

Harvey Holt (Purdue University), T. Davis Sydnor (Ohio State University), Pam Louks (Indiana Community & Urban Forestry Program Coordinator), and Drew Todd (Ohio Department of Natural Resources, Division of Forestry) provided helpful reviews of this work.

Keith Cline and Philip Rodbell (U.S. Department of Agriculture, Forest Service, State and Private Forestry) provided invaluable support for this project.

References

Akbari, H.; Davis, S.; Dorsano, S.; Huang, J.; Winnett, S., eds. 1992. Cooling our communities: a guidebook on tree planting and light-colored surfacing. Washington, DC: U.S. Department of the Interior, Environmental Protection Agency. 26 p.

Alden, H.A. 1995. Hardwoods of North America. Gen. Tech. Rep. 83. Madison, WI: U.S. Department of Agriculture, Forest Service, Forest Products Laboratory. 136 p.

Alliance for Community Trees. 2006. Tree by tree, street by street. http://actrees.org. (27 January 2007).

American Forests. 2002. Urban ecosystem analysis, Benton and Washington Counties, Arkansas: calculating the value of nature. Washington, DC. 12 p.

American Forests. 2004. Urban ecological analysis, Montgomery, AL. Washington, DC. 12 p.

American National Standards Institute. 2008. American National Standards Institute (ANSI), ANSI A300 (Part 1)—2008 American National Standard for tree care operations standard practices (pruning). New York, NY: ANSI. 9 p.

Ames, M.J. 1987. Solar friendly trees report. Portland, OR: City of Portland Energy Office. [Pages unknown].

Anderson, L.M.; Cordell, H.K. 1988. Residential property values improve by landscaping with trees. Southern Journal of Applied Forestry. 9: 162–166.

Bedker, P.J.; O'Brien, J.G.; Mielke, M.E. 1995. How to prune trees. NA-FR-01-95. [Newtown Square, PA]: U.S. Department of Agriculture, Forest Service, Northeastern Area State and Private Forestry. 28 p.

Benjamin, M.T.; Winer, A.M. 1998. Estimating the ozone-forming potential of urban trees and shrubs. Atmospheric Environment. 32: 53–68.

Bernhardt, E.; Swiecki, T.J. 1993. The state of urban forestry in California: results of the 1992 California urban forest survey. Sacramento: California Department of Forestry and Fire Protection. 51 p.

Brandle, J.R.; Nickerson, H.D. 1996. Windbreaks for snow management. EC96-1770-X. Lincoln, NE: University of Nebraska Extension. [Pages unknown].

Bratkovich, S.M. 2001. Utilizing municipal trees: ideas from across the country. NA-TP-06-01. Newtown Square, PA: U.S. Department of Agriculture, Forest Service, Northeastern Area State and Private Forestry. 91 p.

Brenzel, K.N., ed. 2001. Sunset western garden book. 7th ed. Menlo Park, CA: Sunset Books, Inc. 768 p.

Brock, J.H. 1998. Invasion, ecology and management of *Elaeagnus angustifolia* (Russian olive) in the Southwestern U.S.A. In: Starfinger, U.; Edwards, K.; Kowarik, I.; Williamson, M., eds. Plant invasions: ecological mechanisms and human responses. Leiden, The Netherlands: Backhuys Publishers. 372 p.

Brown, B.M. 2007. Personal communication. Professional engineer, AMEC Earth and Environmental, Inc. 101 W Ohio St., Indianapolis, IN 46204.

Cappiella, K.; Schueler, T.; Wright, T. 2005. Urban watershed forestry manual. Ellicott City, MD: Center for Watershed Protection. 138 p.

Cardelino, C.A.; Chameides, W.L. 1990. Natural hydrocarbons, urbanization, and urban ozone. Journal of Geophysical Research. 95(9): 13971–13979.

Chameides, W.L.; Lindsay, R.W.; Richardson, J.; Kiang, C.S. 1988. The role of biogenic hydrocarbons in urban photochemical smog: Atlanta as a case study. Science. 241: 1473–1475.

Chicago Climate Exchange. 2007. About CCX. http://www.chicagoclimatex.com/about/index.html. (21 January 2007).

Citizens Gas and Coke Utility. 2007. Rider A: current gas supply charges. http://www.citizensgas.com/newsinfo/prices.html. (4 May 2007).

CO2e.com. 2007. CO_2e market size and pricing. http://www.co2e.com/strategies/AdditionalInfo.asp?PageID=273#1613. (21 January 2007).

Cook, D.I. 1978. Trees, solid barriers, and combinations: alternatives for noise control. In: Proceedings of the national urban forestry conference. ESF Publ. 80-003. Syracuse, NY: State University of New York: 330–334.

Costello, L.R. 2000. Training young trees for structure and form. [Video] V99-A. Oakland, CA: University of California, Agriculture and Natural Resources, Communication Services Cooperative Extension Service.

Costello, L.R.; Jones, K.S. 2003. Reducing infrastructure damage by tree roots: a compendium of strategies. Cohasset, CA: Western Chapter of the International Society of Arboriculture. 119 p.

Dwyer, J.F.; McPherson, E.G.; Schroeder, H.W.; Rowntree, R.A. 1992. Assessing the benefits and costs of the urban forest. Journal of Arboriculture. 18(5): 227–234.

Dwyer, M.C.; Miller, R.W. 1999. Using GIS to assess urban tree canopy benefits and surrounding greenspace distributions. Journal of Arboriculture. 25(2): 102–107.

European Climate Exchange. 2006. Historic data—ECX CFI futures contract. http://www.europeanclimateexchange.com. (29 August 2006).

Fazio, J.R. [N.d.]. Tree City USA Bulletin Series. Lincoln, NE: The National Arbor Day Foundation.

Geiger, J. 2001. Save dollars with shade. Davis, CA: U.S. Department of Agriculture, Forest Service, Pacific Southwest Research Station. 4 p. http://www.fs.fed.us/psw/programs/cufr/products/3/cufr_149.pdf. (25 January 2007).

Geiger, J. 2002a. Green plants or powerplants? Davis, CA: U.S. Department of Agriculture, Forest Service, Pacific Southwest Research Station. 4 p. http://www.fs.fed.us/psw/programs/cufr/products/3/cufr_148.pdf. (25 January 2007).

Geiger, J. 2002b. Where are all the cool parking lots? Davis, CA: U.S. Department of Agriculture, Forest Service, Pacific Southwest Research Station. 4 p. http://www.fs.fed.us/psw/programs/cufr/products/3/cufr_151.pdf. (25 January 2007).

Geiger, J. 2003. Is all your rain going down the drain? Davis, CA: U.S. Department of Agriculture, Forest Service, Pacific Southwest Research Station. 4 p. http://www.fs.fed.us/psw/programs/cufr/products/cufr_392_rain_down_the_drain.pdf. (25 January 2007).

Geiger, J. 2006. Trees—the air pollution solution. Davis, CA: U.S. Department of Agriculture, Forest Service, Pacific Southwest Research Station. 4 p. http://www.fs.fed.us/psw/programs/cufr/products/3/cufr_658_Air_pollution_solution.pdf. (25 January 2007).

Gilman, E.F. 1997. Trees for urban and suburban landscapes. Albany, NY: Delmar Publishing. 688 p.

Gilman, E.F. 2002. An illustrated guide to pruning. 2nd ed. Albany, NY: Delmar Publishing. 256 p.

Gonzalez, S. 2004. Personal communication. Assistant maintenance superintendent, City of Vallejo, 111 Amador St., Vallejo, CA 94590.

Grant, R.H.; Heisler, G.M.; Goa, W. 2002. Estimation of pedestrian level UV exposure under trees. Photochemistry and Photobiology. 75(4): 369–376.

Guenther, A.B.; Monson, R.K.; Fall, R. 1991. Isoprene and monoterpene emission rate variability: observations with eucalyptus and emission rate algorithm development. Journal of Geophysical Research. 96: 10799–10808.

Guenther, A.B.; Zimmermann, P.R.; Harley, P.C.; Monson, R.K.; Fall, R. 1993. Isoprene and monoterpene emission rate variability: model evaluations and sensitivity analyses. Journal of Geophysical Research. 98: 12609–12617.

Hammer, T.T.; Coughlin, R.; Horn, E. 1974. The effect of a large urban park on real estate value. Journal of the American Institute of Planning: 274–275.

Hammond, J.; Zanetto, J.; Adams, C. 1980. Planning solar neighborhoods. Sacramento, CA: California Energy Commission. 179 p.

Hargrave, R.; Johnson, G.R.; Zins, M.E. 2002. Planting trees and shrubs for long-term health. MI-07681-S. St. Paul, MN: University of Minnesota Extension Service. 12 p.

Harris, R.W.; Clark, J.R.; Matheny, N.P. 2003. Arboriculture. 4th ed. Englewood Cliffs, NJ: Regents/Prentice Hall. 592 p.

Hauer, R.J.; Hruska, M.C.; Dawson, J.O. 1994. Trees and ice storms: the development of ice storm-resistant urban tree populations. Special Publ. 94-1. Urbana, IL: Department of Forestry, University of Illinois at Urbana-Champaign. 12 p.

Haugen, L.M. 1998. How to identify and manage Dutch elm disease. NA-PR-07-98. [Newtown Square, PA]: U.S. Department of Agriculture, Forest Service, Northeastern Area State and Private Forestry. 26 p.

Heisler, G.M. 1986. Energy savings with trees. Journal of Arboriculture. 12(5): 113–125.

Hightshoe, G.L. 1988. Native trees, shrubs, and vines for urban and rural America. New York: Van Nostrand Reinhold. 832 p.

Hildebrandt, E.W.; Kallett, R.; Sarkovich, M.; Sequest, R. 1996. Maximizing the energy benefits of urban forestation. In: Proceedings of the ACEEE 1996 summer study on energy efficiency in buildings. Washington, DC: American Council for an Energy Efficient Economy: 121–131. Vol. 9.

Hudson, B. 1983. Private sector business analogies applied in urban forestry. Journal of Arboriculture. 9(10): 253–258.

Hull, R.B. 1992. How the public values urban forests. Journal of Arboriculture. 18(2): 98–101.

Indianapolis Power and Light Company. 2007. I.U.R.C. No. E-16. Rate RS residential service electricity rates. http://www.aes.com/pub-sites/IPL/content/staging/0205017431b9010a483052b3006d66/resident.pdf. (17 May 2007.)

Intergovernmental Panel on Climate Change [IPCC]. 2007. Climate change 2007: synthesis report. Valencia, Spain. 52 p.

International Society of Arboriculture [ISA]. 1992. Avoiding tree and utility conflicts. Savoy, IL. 4 p.

International Society of Arboriculture [ISA]. 2006. Welcome to the International Society of Arboriculture. http://www.isa-arbor.com/home.aspx. (27 January 2007).

Jo, H.K.; McPherson, E.G. 1995. Carbon storage and flux in residential greenspace. Journal of Environmental Management. 45: 109–133.

Kaplan, R. 1992. Urban forestry and the workplace. In: Gobster, P.H., ed. Managing urban and high-use recreation settings. Gen. Tech. Rep. NC-163. St. Paul, MN: U.S. Department of Agriculture, Forest Service, North Central Research Station: 41–45.

Kaplan, R.; Kaplan, S. 1989. The experience of nature: a psychological perspective. Cambridge, United Kingdom: Cambridge University Press. 360 p.

Kim, S.; Byun, D.W.; Cheng, F.-Y.; Czader, B.; Stetson, S.; Nowak, D.; Walton, J.; Estes, M.; Hitchcock, D. 2005. Modeling effects of land use land cover changes on meteorology and air quality in Houston, Texas, over the last two decades. In: Proceedings of the 2005 atmospheric sciences air quality conference. http://ams.confex.com/ams/pdfpapers/92244.pdf. (23 January 2007).

Lewis, C.A. 1996. Green nature/human nature: the meaning of plants in our lives. Chicago, IL: University of Illinois Press. 176 p.

Luley, C.J.; Bond, J. 2002. A plan to integrate management of urban trees into air quality planning. Naples, NY: Davey Resource Group. 61 p.

Maco, S.E.; McPherson, E.G. 2003. A practical approach to assessing structure, function, and value of street tree populations in small communities. Journal of Arboriculture. 29(2): 84–97.

Marion, W.; Urban, K. 1995. User's manual for TMY2s—typical meteorological years. Golden, CO: National Renewable Energy Laboratory. 49 p.

Markwardt, L.J. 1930. Comparative strength properties of woods grown in the United States. Tech. Bull. 158. Washington, DC: U.S. Department of Agriculture. 38 p.

McHale, M. 2003. Carbon credit markets: Is there a role for community forestry? In: Kollin, C., ed. 2003 national urban forest conference proceedings. Washington, DC: American Forests: 74–77.

McHale, M. [In press]. Volume equations for 11 urban tree species in Fort Collins, CO: Urban Forestry and Urban Greening.

McKenzie, D.; Gedalof, Z.; Peterson, D.L.; Mote, P. 2004. Climate change, wildfire, and conservation. Conservation Biology. 18(4): 890–902.

McPherson, E.G. 1984. Planting design for solar control. In: McPherson, E.G., ed. Energy-conserving site design. Washington, DC: American Society of Landscape Architects: 141–164. Chapter 8.

McPherson, E.G. 1992. Accounting for benefits and costs of urban greenspace. Landscape and Urban Planning. 22: 41–51.

McPherson, E.G. 1993. Evaluating the cost effectiveness of shade trees for demand-side management. The Electricity Journal. 6(9): 57–65.

McPherson, E.G. 1995. Net benefits of healthy and productive forests. In: Bradley, G.A., ed. Urban forest landscapes: integrating multidisciplinary perspectives. Seattle, WA: University of Washington Press: 180–194.

McPherson, E.G. 2000. Expenditures associated with conflicts between street tree root growth and hardscape in California. Journal of Arboriculture. 26(6): 289–297.

McPherson, E.G. 2001. Sacramento's parking lot shading ordinance: environmental and economic costs of compliance. Landscape and Urban Planning. 57: 105–123.

McPherson, E.G.; Mathis, S., eds. 1999. Proceedings of the best of the West summit. Sacramento, CA: International Society of Arboriculture, Western Chapter. 93 p.

McPherson, E.G.; Muchnick, J. 2005. Effects of tree shade on asphalt concrete pavement performance. Journal of Arboriculture. 31(6): 303–309.

McPherson, E.G.; Nowak, D.J.; Heisler, G.; Grimmond, S.; Souch, C.; Grant, R.; Rowntree, R.A. 1997. Quantifying urban forest structure, function, and value: Chicago's Urban Forest Climate Project. Urban Ecosystems. 1: 49–61.

McPherson, E.G.; Nowak, D.J.; Rowntree, R.A. 1994. Chicago's urban forest ecosystem: results of the Chicago Urban Forest Climate Project. Gen. Tech. Rep. NE-186. Radnor [Newtown Square], PA: U.S. Department of Agriculture, Forest Service, Northeastern Research Station. 201 p.

McPherson, E.G.; Peper, P.J. 1995. Infrastructure repair costs associated with street trees in 15 cities. In: Watson, G.W.; Neely, D., eds. Trees and building sites. Champaign, IL: International Society of Arboriculture: 49–63.

McPherson, E.G.; Sacamano, P.L.; Wensman, S. 1993. Modeling benefits and costs of community tree plantings. Albany, CA: U.S. Department of Agriculture, Forest Service, Pacific Southwest Research Station. 170 p.

McPherson, E.G.; Simpson, J.R. 1999. Carbon dioxide reduction through urban forestry: guidelines for professional and volunteer tree planters. Gen. Tech. Rep. PSW-171. Albany, CA: U.S. Department of Agriculture, Forest Service, Pacific Southwest Research Station. 237 p.

McPherson, E.G.; Simpson, J.R. 2002. A comparison of municipal forest benefits and costs in Modesto and Santa Monica, CA, USA. Urban Forestry and Urban Greening. 1: 61–74.

McPherson, E.G.; Simpson, J.R. 2003. Potential energy savings in buildings by an urban tree planting programme in California. Urban Forestry and Urban Greening. 2(2): 73–86.

McPherson, E.G.; Simpson, J.R.; Peper, P.J.; Gardner, S.L.; Vargas, K.E.; Maco, S.E.; Xiao, Q. 2006a. Coastal Plain community tree guide: benefits, costs, and strategic planting. Gen. Tech. Rep. PSW-GTR-201. Albany, CA: U.S. Department of Agriculture, Forest Service, Pacific Southwest Research Station. 99 p.

McPherson, E.G.; Simpson, J.R.; Peper, P.J.; Gardner, S.L.; Vargas, K.E.; Maco, S.E.; Xiao, Q. 2006b. Piedmont community tree guide: benefits, costs, and strategic planting. Gen Tech. Rep. PSW-GTR-200. Albany, CA: U.S. Department of Agriculture, Forest Service, Pacific Southwest Research Station. 95 p.

McPherson, E.G.; Simpson, J.R.; Peper, P.J.; Gardner, S.L.; Vargas, K.E.; Xiao, Q. 2007. Northeast community tree guide: benefits, costs, and strategic planting. Gen. Tech. Rep. PSW-GTR-202. Albany, CA: U.S. Department of Agriculture, Forest Service, Pacific Southwest Research Station. 102 p.

McPherson, E.G.; Simpson, J.R.; Peper, P.J.; Maco, S.E.; Gardner, S.L.; Cozad, S.K.; Xiao, Q. 2006c. Midwest community tree guide: benefits, costs, and strategic planting. Gen. Tech. Rep. PSW-GTR-199. Albany, CA: U.S. Department of Agriculture, Forest Service, Pacific Southwest Research Station. 85 p.

McPherson, E.G.; Simpson, J.R.; Peper, P.J.; Maco, S.E.; Xiao, Q.; Hoefer, P.J. 2003. Northern mountain and prairie community tree guide: benefits, costs, and strategic planting. Albany, CA: U.S. Department of Agriculture, Forest Service, Pacific Southwest Research Station. 88 p.

McPherson, E.G.; Simpson, J.R.; Peper, P.J.; Maco, S.E.; Xiao, Q.; Mulrean, E. 2004. Desert Southwest community tree guide: benefits, costs, and strategic planting. Albany, CA: U.S. Department of Agriculture, Forest Service, Pacific Southwest Research Station. 65 p.

McPherson, E.G.; Simpson, J.R.; Peper, P.J.; Scott, K.; Xiao, Q. 2000. Tree guidelines for coastal southern California communities. Sacramento, CA: Local Government Commission. 97 p.

McPherson, E.G.; Simpson, J.R.; Peper, P.J.; Xiao, Q. 1999a. Benefit-cost analysis of Modesto's municipal urban forest. Journal of Arboriculture. 25(5): 235–248.

McPherson, E.G.; Simpson, J.R.; Peper, P.J.; Xiao, Q. 1999b. Tree guidelines for San Joaquin Valley communities. Sacramento, CA: Local Government Commission. 63 p.

Metro. 2002. Green streets: innovative solutions for stormwater and stream crossings. Portland, OR. 144 p.

Midwest Invasive Plant Network. 2006. Invasive plants in the Midwest. http://mipn.org/New%20Invasives%20Flyer.pdf. (7 April 2008).

Miller, R.W. 1997. Urban forestry: planning and managing urban greenspaces. 2^d ed. Upper Saddle River, NJ: Prentice-Hall. 502 p.

More, T.A.; Stevens, T.; Allen, P.G. 1988. Valuation of urban parks. Landscape and Urban Planning. 15: 139–152.

Morgan, R. [N.d.]. An introductory guide to community and urban forestry in Washington, Oregon, and California. Portland, OR: World Forestry Center. 25 p.

Morgan, R. 1993. A technical guide to urban and community forestry. Portland, OR: World Forestry Center. 49 p.

National Arbor Day Foundation. 2006. Color your world. http://www.arborday.org. (27 January 2007).

Neely, D., ed. 1988. Valuation of landscape trees, shrubs, and other plants. 7th ed. Urbana, IL: International Society of Arboriculture. 50 p.

Noble, R.D.; Martin, J.L.; Jensen, K.F., eds. 1988. Air pollution effects on vegetation, including forest ecosystems. Proceedings of the second US–USSR symposium. Gov. Doc. A13.42/2:2:A:7. Broomall [Newtown Square], PA: U.S. Department of Agriculture, Forest Service, Northeastern Research Station. 311 p.

Nowak, D.J. 1994. Air pollution removal by Chicago's urban forest. In: McPherson, E.G.; Nowak, D.J.; Rowntree, R.A., eds. Chicago's urban forest ecosystem: results of the Chicago urban forest climate project. Gen. Tech. Rep. NE-186. Radnor [Newtown Square], PA: U.S. Department of Agriculture, Forest Service, Northeastern Research Station: 63–82.

Nowak, D.J. 2000. Tree species selection, design, and management to improve air quality. In: Scheu, D.L., ed. 2000 ASLA annual meeting proceedings. Washington, DC: American Society of Landscape Architects: 23–27.

Nowak, D.J.; Civerolo, K.L.; Rao, S.T.; Sistla, G.; Luley, C.J.; Crane, D.E. 2000. A modeling study of the impact of urban trees on ozone. Atmospheric Environment. 34: 1601–1613.

Nowak, D.J.; Crane, D.E. 2002. Carbon storage and sequestration by urban trees in the USA. Environmental Pollution. 116: 381–389.

Nowak, D.J.; Hoehn, R.; Crane, D.E. 2007. Oxygen production by urban trees in the United States. Arboriculture and Urban Forestry. 33(3): 220–226.

Ottinger, R.L.; Wooley, D.R.; Robinson, N.A.; Hodas, D.R.; Babb, S.E. 1990. Environmental costs of electricity. New York: Oceana Publications. 769 p.

Parsons, R.; Tassinary, L.G.; Ulrich, R.S.; Hebl, M.R.; Grossman-Alexander, M. 1998. The view from the road: implications for stress recovery and immunization. Journal of Environmental Psychology. 18(2): 113–140.

Pearce, D. 2003. The social cost of carbon and its policy implications. Oxford Review of Public Policy. 19(3): 362–384.

Peper, P.J.; McPherson, E.G. 2003. Evaluation of four methods for estimating leaf area of isolated trees. Urban Forestry and Urban Greening. 2(1): 19–29.

Peper, P.J.; McPherson, E.G.; Simpson, J.R.; Vargas, K.E.; Xiao, Q. 2008. City of Indianapolis, Indiana, Municipal Forest Resource Analysis. Internal Tech. Rep. Davis, CA: U.S. Department of Agriculture, Forest Service, Pacific Southwest Research Station, Center for Urban Forest Research. 68 p.

Perry, J.; LeVan, M.D. c. 2003. Air purification in closed environments: overview of spacecraft systems. U.S. Army Natick Soldier Center. http://nsc.natick.army.mil/jocotas/ColPro_Papers/Perry-LeVan.pdf. (June 2008).

Pillsbury, N.H.; Reimer, J.L.; Thompson, R.P. 1998. Tree volume equations for fifteen urban species in California. Tech. Rep. 7. San Luis Obispo, CA: Urban Forest Ecosystems Institute, California Polytechnic State University. 56 p.

Pinco, P. 2007. Personal communication. City arborist, Indy Parks and Recreation Department, Forestry Section, 6820 E 32 St., Indianapolis, IN 46226.

Platt, R.H.; Rowntree, R.A.; Muick, P.C., eds. 1994. The ecological city. Boston, MA: University of Massachusetts. 292 p.

Pokorny, J.D., ed. 2003. Urban tree risk management: a community guide to program design and implementation. NA-TP-03-03. Newtown Square, PA: U.S. Department of Agriculture, Forest Service, Northeastern Area State and Private Forestry. [Pages unknown].

Ramsay, S. 2002. Personal communication. Executive Director, Trees Forever, 770 7th Ave., Marion, IA 52302.

Ray, C. 2007. Indianapolis takes on the largest investment in clean-water infrastructure in city history. Stormwater. 8(5): 12–14.

Richards, N.A.; Mallette, J.R.; Simpson, R.J.; Macie, E.A. 1984. Residential greenspace and vegetation in a mature city: Syracuse, New York. Urban Ecology. 8: 99–125.

Rosenzweig, C.; Solecki, W.; Parshall, L.; Hodges, S. 2006. Mitigating New York City's heat island with urban forestry, living roofs, and light surfaces. New York City regional heat island initiative final report 06-06. Albany, NY: New York State Energy Research and Development Authority. 173 p.

Sand, M. 1991. Planting for energy conservation in the North. Minneapolis, MN: Minnesota Department of Natural Resources. 19 p.

Sand, M. 1993. Energy saving landscapes: the Minnesota homeowner's guide. Minneapolis, MN: Minnesota Department of Natural Resources. [Pages unknown].

Sand, M. 1994. Design and species selection to reduce urban heat island and conserve energy. In: Proceedings from the 6th national urban forest conference: growing greener communities. Washington, DC: American Forests. 282 p.

Schroeder, H.W.; Cannon, W.N. 1983. The esthetic contribution of trees to residential streets in Ohio towns. Journal of Arboriculture. 9: 237–243.

Schroeder, T. 1982. The relationship of local park and recreation services to residential property values. Journal of Leisure Research. 14: 223–234.

Scott, K.I.; McPherson, E.G.; Simpson, J.R. 1998. Air pollutant uptake by Sacramento's urban forest. Journal of Arboriculture. 24(4): 224–234.

Scott, K.I.; Simpson, J.R.; McPherson, E.G. 1999. Effects of tree cover on parking lot microclimate and vehicle emissions. Journal of Arboriculture. 25(3): 129–142.

Simpson, J.R. 1998. Urban forest impacts on regional space conditioning energy use: Sacramento County case study. Journal of Arboriculture. 24(4): 201–214.

Smith, W.H. 1990. Air pollution and forests. New York: Springer-Verlag. 618 p.

Smith, W.H.; Dochinger, L.S. 1976. Capability of metropolitan trees to reduce atmospheric contaminants. In: Santamour, F.S.; Gerhold, H.D.; Little, S., eds. Better trees for metropolitan landscapes. Gen. Tech. Rep. NE-22. Upper Darby [Newtown Square], PA: U.S. Department of Agriculture, Forest Service, Northeastern Research Station: 49–60.

Sullivan, W.C.; Kuo, E.E. 1996. Do trees strengthen urban communities, reduce domestic violence? Arborist News. 5(2): 33–34.

Summit, J.; McPherson, E.G. 1998. Residential tree planting and care: a study of attitudes and behavior in Sacramento, California. Journal of Arboriculture. 24(2): 89–97.

Sydnor, T.D.; Gamstetter, D.; Nichols, J.; Bishop, B.; Favorite, J.; Blazer, C.; Turpin, L. 2000. Trees are not the root of sidewalk problems. Journal of Arboriculture. 26: 20–29.

Taha, H. 1996. Modeling impacts of increased urban vegetation on ozone air quality in the South Coast Air Basin. Atmospheric Environment. 30: 3423–3430.

Ter-Mikaelian, M.T.; Korzukhin, M.D. 1997. Biomass equations for sixty-five North American tree species. Forest Ecology and Management. 97: 1–24.

Thompson, R.P.; Ahern, J.J. 2000. The state of urban and community forestry in California. San Luis Obispo, CA: Urban Forest Ecosystems Institute, California Polytechnic State University. 48 p.

Treelink. 2007. Improving urban and community forests by providing Internet-based information, tools, and inspiration. http://www.treelink.org. (29 June 2007).

Tretheway, R.; Manthe, A. 1999. Skin cancer prevention: another good reason to plant trees. In: McPherson, E.G.; Mathis, S. Proceedings of the best of the West summit. Davis, CA: University of California: 72–75.

Tritton, L.M.; Hornbeck, J.W. 1982. Biomass equations for major tree species of the Northeast. Gen. Tech. Rep. No. 69. Broomall, PA: U.S. Department of Agriculture, Forest Service, Northeast Research Station. 46 p.

Tschantz, B.A.; Sacamano, P.L. 1994. Municipal tree management in the United States. Kent, OH: Davey Resource Group. 71 p.

Tyrvainen, L. 1999. Monetary valuation of urban forest amenities in Finland. Res. Pap. 739. Vantaa, Finland: Finnish Forest Research Institute. 129 p.

Ulrich, R.S. 1985. Human responses to vegetation and landscapes. Landscape and Urban Planning. 13: 29–44.

Urban Horticulture Institute. 2003. Recommended urban trees: site assessment and tree selection for stress tolerance. http://www.hort.cornell.edu/UHI/outreach/recurbtree/index.html. (7 February 2007).

Urban, J. 1992. Bringing order to the technical dysfunction within the urban forest. Journal of Arboriculture. 18(2): 85–90.

U.S. Department of Agriculture, Forest Service [USDA FS]. 2006a. i-Tree: tools for assessing and managing community forests. http://www.itreetools.org. (27 January 2007).

U.S. Department of Agriculture, Forest Service [USDA FS]. 2006b. Urban tree cover and air quality planning. http://www.treescleanair.org. (21 January 2007).

U.S. Department of Agriculture, Natural Resource Conservation Service, Agroforestry Center [USDA NRCS Agroforesty Center]. 2005. Working trees for treating waste. Western Arborist. 31: 50–52.

U.S. Department of Agriculture, Soil Conservation Service [USDA SCS]. 1986. Urban hydrology for small watersheds. Technical Release 55. 2nd ed. Washington, DC. 164 p.

U.S. Department of Commerce, Census Bureau. 2006. State and county quick facts. http://quickfacts.census.gov/qfd/index.html. (March 2006).

U.S. Department of Transportation. 1995. Highway traffic noise analysis and abatement policy and guidance. Washington, DC: Federal Highway Administration. 67 p.

U.S. Department of the Interior, Environmental Protection Agency [US EPA]. 1998. Ap-42 Compilation of air pollutant emission factors. 5th ed. Research Triangle Park, NC. [Pages unknown.] Volume I.

**U.S. Department of the Interior, Environmental Protection Agency [US EPA].
2003.** E-GRID (E-GRID2002 Edition). http://www.epa.gov/cleanenergy/egrid/
index.htm. (6 December 2006).

**U.S. Department of the Interior, Environmental Protection Agency [US EPA].
2006.** Green book: nonattainment areas for criteria pollutants. http://
www.epa.gov/air/oaqps/greenbk/index.html. (6 December 2006).

**U.S. Department of the Interior, Environmental Protection Agency [US EPA].
2007.** Technology transfer network air quality system. http://www.epa.gov/ttn/
airs/airsaqs/detaildata/datarequest.html. (21 May 2007).

van Rentergehm, T.; Botteldooren, D.; Cornelis, W.M.; Gabriels, D. 2002.
Reducing screen-induced refraction of noise barriers in wind by vegetative
screens. Acta Acustica United with Acustica. 88: 231–238.

**Vargas, K.E.; McPherson, E.G.; Simpson, J.R.; Peper, P.J.; Gardner, S.L.;
Xiao, Q. 2006.** City of Albuquerque, New Mexico, municipal forest resource
analysis. Internal Tech. Rep. Davis, CA: U.S. Department of Agriculture,
Forest Service, Pacific Southwest Research Station, Center for Urban Forest
Research. 51 p.

**Vargas, K.E.; McPherson, E.G.; Simpson, J.R.; Peper, P.J.; Gardner, S.L.;
Xiao, Q. 2007a.** Interior West community tree guide: benefits, costs, and
strategic planting. Gen. Tech. Rep. PSW-GTR-205. Albany, CA: U.S. Department of Agriculture, Forest Service, Pacific Southwest Research Station. 105 p.

**Vargas, K.E.; McPherson, E.G.; Simpson J.R.; Peper, P.J.; Gardner, S.L.;
Xiao, Q. 2007b.** Temperate interior West community tree guide: benefits,
costs, and strategic planting. Gen. Tech. Rep. PSW-GTR-206. Albany, CA:
U.S. Department of Agriculture, Forest Service, Pacific Southwest Research
Station. 108 p.

Wang, M.Q.; Santini, D.J. 1995. Monetary values of air pollutant emissions in
various U.S. regions. Transportation Research Record. 1475: 33–41.

Watson, G.W.; Himelick, E.B. 1997. Principles and practice of planting trees and
shrubs. Savoy, IL: International Society of Arboriculture. 199 p.

Wolf, K.L. 1999. Nature and commerce: human ecology in business districts. In: Kollin, C., ed. Building cities of green: proceedings of the 1999 national urban forest conference. Washington, DC: American Forests: 56–59.

Xiao, Q.; McPherson, E.G. 2002. Rainfall interception by Santa Monica's municipal urban forest. Urban Ecosystems. 6: 291–302.

Xiao, Q.; McPherson, E.G.; Simpson, J.R.; Ustin, S.L. 1998. Rainfall interception by Sacramento's urban forest. Journal of Arboriculture. 24(4): 235–244.

Xiao, Q.; McPherson, E.G.; Simpson, J.R.; Ustin, S.L. 2000. Winter rainfall interception by two mature open grown trees in Davis, California. Hydrological Processes. 14(4): 763–784.

Appendix 1: Additional Resources

Additional information regarding urban and community forestry program design and implementation can be obtained from the following sources:

Utilizing Municipal Trees: Ideas From Across the Country by S.M. Bratkovich

Urban Forestry: Planning and Managing Urban Greenspaces by R.W. Miller

An Introductory Guide to Community and Urban Forestry in Washington, Oregon, and California by N.R. Morgan

A Technical Guide to Urban and Community Forestry by N.R. Morgan

Urban Tree Risk Management: A Community Guide to Program Design and Implementation edited by J.D. Pokorny

For additional information on tree selection, planting, establishment, and care see the following resources:

Alliance for Community Trees: http://actrees.org

How to Prune Trees by P.J. Bedker, J.G. O'Brien, and M.E. Mielke

Training Young Trees for Structure and Form, a video by L.R. Costello

An Illustrated Guide to Pruning by E.F. Gilman

Planting Trees and Shrubs for Long-Term Health by R. Hargrave, G.R. Johnson, and M.E. Zins

Arboriculture. 4th ed. by R.W. Harris, J.R. Clark, and N.P. Matheny

Trees and Ice Storms: The Development of Ice Storm-Resistant Urban Tree Populations by R.J. Hauer, M.C. Hruska, and J.O. Dawson

How to Identify and Manage Dutch Elm Disease by L.M. Haugen

Native Trees, Shrubs, and Vines for Urban and Rural America by G.L. Hightshoe

International Society of Arboriculture: http://www.isa-arbor.com, including their *Tree City USA Bulletin* series by J.R. Fazio

National Arbor Day Foundation: http://www.arborday.org

TreeLink: http://www.treelink.org

Trees for Urban and Suburban Landscapes by E.F. Gilman

The Urban Horticulture Institute: http://www.hort.cornell.edu/UHI/outreach/recurbtree/index.html

Principles and Practice of Planting Trees and Shrubs by G.W. Watson and E.B. Himelick

State urban forestry agencies and Web sites for the lower Midwest region:

Arkansas Forestry Commission, Community Forestry, 2780 North Garland Avenue, Fayetteville, AR 72704; Phone: 479-442-8627 http://www.forestry.state.ar.us/community/community.html

Illinois Department of Natural Resources, Urban Conservation Program, One Natural Resources Way, Springfield, IL 62702; Phone: 217-785-8771 http://dnr.state.il.us/conservation/forestry/Urban/

Indiana DNR, Division of Forestry, Urban Forestry Program, 6515 E 82nd Street, Ste 204, Indianapolis, IN 46250; Phone: 317-915-9390, Fax: 317-915-9392 http://www.in.gov/dnr/forestry/6991.htm

Kansas Forest Service, Community Forestry, 1901 East 95 Street South, Haysville, KS 67060; Phone: 316-788-0492 http://www.kansasforests.org/community/index.shtml

Kentucky Division of Forestry, Urban Forestry, 627 Comanche Trail, Frankfort, KY 40601; Phone: 502-564-4496 http://www.forestry.ky.gov/programs/urban/

Missouri Department of Conservation, Urban and Community Forestry, P.O. Box 180, Jefferson City, MO 65102; Phone: 573-751-4115 x 3116 http://mdc4.mdc.mo.gov/applications/MDCLibrary/MDCLibrary2.aspx?NodeID=147

Division of Forestry, Urban Forestry, 2045 Morse Road, Bldg. H-1, Columbus, OH 43229; Phone: 614-265-6707 http://www.dnr.state.oh.us/forestry/Home/urban/defaultbu/tabid/5438/Default.aspx

Oklahoma Department of Agriculture, Forestry Division, Urban Forestry, 2800 N Lincoln Blvd., Oklahoma City, OK 73105; Phone: 405-522-6150; http://www.forestry.ok.gov/ucf

These suggested references are only a starting point. Your local cooperative extension agent or urban forester can provide you with up-to-date and local information.

Appendix 2: Benefit–Cost Information Tables

Information in this appendix can be used to estimate benefits and costs associated with proposed tree plantings. The tables contain data for representative small (eastern redbud), medium (littleleaf linden), and large (northern hackberry) deciduous trees (see "Common and Scientific Names" section). Data are presented as annual values for each 5-year interval after planting (tables 6 to 14). Annual values incorporate effects of tree loss. Based on the results of our survey, we assume that 50 percent of the trees planted die by the end of the 40-year period.

For the benefits tables (tables 6, 9, 12), there are two columns for each 5-year interval. In the first column, values describe **resource units** (RUs): for example, the amount of air conditioning energy saved in kilowatt hours per year per tree, air pollutant uptake in pounds per year per tree, and rainfall intercepted in gallons per year per tree. Energy and carbon dioxide benefits for residential yard trees are broken out by tree location to show how shading effects differ among trees opposite west-, south-, and east-facing building walls. The second column for each 5-year interval contains dollar values obtained by multiplying RUs by local prices (e.g., kWh saved [RU] x $/kWh).

In the costs tables (tables 7, 10, 13), costs are broken down into categories for yard and public trees. Costs for yard trees do not differ by planting location (i.e., east, west, south walls). Although tree purchase and planting costs occur at year 1, we divided this value by 5 years to derive an average annual cost for the first 5-year period. All other costs are the estimated values for each year and not values averaged over 5 years.

Total net benefits are calculated by subtracting total costs from total benefits and are presented in tables 8, 11, and 14. Data are presented for a yard tree opposite west-, south-, and east-facing walls, as well as for the public tree.

The last column in each table presents 40-year-average annual values. These numbers were calculated by dividing the total costs and benefits by 40 years.

Table 6—Annual benefits at 5-year intervals and 40-year average for a representative small tree (eastern redbud)

	Year 5		Year 10		Year 15		Year 20		Year 25		Year 30		Year 35		Year 40		40-year average	
	RU	$	RU	$	RU	$	RU	$	RU	$	RU	$	RU	$	RU	$	RU	$
Cooling (kWh):																		
Yard: west	14	0.94	35	2.36	55	3.73	72	4.93	83	5.65	90	6.11	91	6.19	91	6.16	66	4.51
Yard: south	8	0.57	17	1.15	26	1.76	34	2.30	38	2.62	41	2.81	42	2.84	41	2.81	31	2.11
Yard: east	9	0.64	20	1.39	33	2.22	43	2.96	50	3.39	54	3.65	54	3.69	54	3.66	40	2.70
Public	8	0.56	17	1.13	24	1.66	31	2.12	35	2.39	38	2.57	38	2.59	38	2.57	29	1.95
Heating (therms):																		
Yard: west	0.14	0.14	0.12	0.12	-0.01	-0.01	-0.15	-0.14	-0.26	-0.25	-0.36	-0.35	-0.41	-0.40	-0.44	-0.43	-0.17	(0.16)
Yard: south	-0.10	-0.09	-0.91	-0.89	-2.30	-2.24	-3.65	-3.55	-4.57	-4.45	-5.28	-5.14	-5.56	-5.41	-5.68	-5.53	-3.51	(3.41)
Yard: east	0.19	0.19	0.22	0.22	0.11	0.10	-0.03	-0.03	-0.13	-0.13	-0.23	-0.22	-0.28	-0.28	-0.32	-0.31	-0.06	(0.06)
Public	0.44	0.43	0.97	0.94	1.36	1.32	1.67	1.62	1.83	1.78	1.92	1.87	1.91	1.85	1.86	1.81	1.49	1.45
Net energy (kWh):																		
Yard: west	152	1.07	359	2.48	548	3.72	710	4.78	805	5.40	863	5.76	870	5.80	862	5.73	646	4.34
Yard: south	74	0.47	77	0.26	28	-0.49	-27	-1.25	-72	-1.83	-115	-2.33	-138	-2.57	-154	-2.72	-41	(1.31)
Yard: east	113	0.83	227	1.61	337	2.32	432	2.93	485	3.26	513	3.42	514	3.41	506	3.35	391	2.64
Public	127	0.99	263	2.07	380	2.98	478	3.74	535	4.18	569	4.43	572	4.45	564	4.38	436	3.40
Net carbon dioxide (lb):																		
Yard: west	33	0.11	83	0.28	130	0.43	171	0.57	194	0.65	206	0.69	206	0.69	203	0.68	153	0.51
Yard: south	19	0.06	32	0.11	39	0.13	46	0.15	46	0.15	42	0.14	38	0.13	34	0.11	37	0.12
Yard: east	25	0.08	53	0.18	83	0.28	109	0.37	123	0.41	128	0.43	127	0.43	125	0.42	97	0.32
Public	25	0.08	53	0.18	79	0.27	102	0.34	114	0.38	119	0.40	118	0.39	115	0.38	91	0.30
Air pollution (lb)[a]																		
Ozone uptake	0.039	0.03	0.094	0.08	0.143	0.12	0.191	0.16	0.230	0.19	0.266	0.22	0.292	0.24	0.319	0.26	0.20	0.16
Nitrogen dioxide uptake+avoided	0.039	0.03	0.086	0.07	0.129	0.11	0.168	0.14	0.193	0.16	0.210	0.17	0.216	0.18	0.220	0.18	0.16	0.13
Sulfur dioxide uptake+avoided	0.125	0.19	0.280	0.42	0.435	0.65	0.571	0.86	0.654	0.98	0.708	1.06	0.720	1.08	0.719	1.08	0.53	0.79
Small particulate matter uptake+avoided	0.020	0.02	0.066	0.07	0.125	0.12	0.187	0.19	0.193	0.19	0.197	0.20	0.198	0.20	0.197	0.20	0.15	0.15
Volatile organic compounds avoided	0.010	0.00	0.022	0.01	0.034	0.01	0.045	0.01	0.051	0.02	0.055	0.02	0.056	0.02	0.055	0.02	0.04	0.01
Biogenic volatile organic compounds released	0.000	0.00	0.000	0.00	0.000	0.00	0.000	0.00	0.000	0.00	0.000	0.00	0.000	0.00	0.000	0.00	0.00	0.00
Total air pollution avoided + net uptake	0.233	0.28	0.548	0.64	0.866	1.01	1.162	1.35	1.321	1.54	1.435	1.67	1.482	1.71	1.510	1.73	1.07	1.24
Hydrology (gal)																		
Rainfall interception	167	1.03	516	3.20	814	5.04	1,101	6.83	1,325	8.22	1,521	9.43	1,667	10.34	1,814	11.25	1,116	6.92
Aesthetics and other:																		
Yard		14.59		12.17		10.03		7.95		6.06		4.41		3.04		1.94		7.52
Public		16.45		13.73		11.31		8.97		6.83		4.97		3.42		2.19		8.48
Total benefits:																		
Yard: west		17.08		18.77		20.24		21.48		21.85		21.95		21.57		21.33		20.53
Yard: south		16.43		16.38		15.73		15.03		14.13		13.31		12.65		12.32		14.50
Yard: east		16.80		17.80		18.68		19.43		19.48		19.35		18.92		18.68		18.64
Public		18.83		19.82		20.61		21.23		21.14		20.89		20.31		19.93		20.35

Note: Annual values incorporate effects of tree loss. We assume that 10 percent of trees planted die during the first 5 years and 40 percent during the remaining 35 years for a total mortality of 50 percent. RU = resource unit.

[a] Values are the same for yard and public trees.

Table 7—Annual costs (dollars per tree) at 5-year intervals and 40-year average for a representative small tree (eastern redbud)

Costs	Year 5	Year 10	Year 15	Year 20	Year 25	Year 30	Year 35	Year 40	40-year average
					Dollars				
Tree and planting[a]:									
Yard	32								4
Public	31								3.88
Pruning:									
Yard	0.29	0.56	0.54	0.52	4.06	3.92	3.79	3.65	2.20
Public	6.56	3.33	3.16	2.99	5.28	4.96	4.63	4.31	4.54
Remove and dispose:									
Yard	0.64	0.99	1.48	1.95	2.39	2.79	3.14	3.42	1.95
Public	0.40	0.90	1.35	1.77	2.18	2.54	2.86	3.12	1.74
Pest and disease:									
Yard	0.02	0.05	0.07	0.09	0.10	0.11	0.12	0.13	0.08
Public	0.03	0.06	0.09	0.11	0.12	0.13	0.14	0.14	0.10
Infrastructure repair:									
Yard	0.05	0.09	0.14	0.17	0.21	0.23	0.25	0.27	0.16
Public	0.35	0.67	0.95	1.19	1.37	1.50	1.58	1.60	1.08
Irrigation:									
Yard	0.00	0.00	0.00	0.00	0.00	0.00	0.00	0.00	0.00
Public	1.75	0.00	0.00	0.00	0.00	0.00	0.00	0.00	0.23
Cleanup:									
Yard	0.03	0.06	0.09	0.12	0.14	0.16	0.17	0.18	0.11
Public	0.24	0.46	0.66	0.82	0.95	1.04	1.09	1.11	0.74
Liability and legal:									
Yard	0.00	0.00	0.00	0.01	0.01	0.01	0.01	0.01	0.01
Public	0.01	0.02	0.03	0.04	0.04	0.05	0.05	0.05	0.03
Admin./inspect/other:									
Yard	0.00	0.00	0.00	0.00	0.00	0.00	0.00	0.00	0.00
Public	1.26	2.41	3.42	4.26	4.93	5.40	5.68	5.77	3.87
Total costs:									
Yard	33.03	1.75	2.32	2.86	6.91	7.23	7.48	7.66	8.50
Public	41.61	7.85	9.64	11.17	14.87	15.62	16.04	16.10	16.20

Note: Annual values incorporate effects of tree loss. We assume that 10 percent of trees planted die during the first 5 years and 40 percent during the remaining 35 years for a total mortality of 50 percent.

[a] Although tree and planting costs occur in year 1, this value was divided by 5 years to derive an average annual cost for the first 5-year period.

Table 8—Annual net benefits (dollars per tree) at 5-year intervals and 40-year average for a representative small tree (eastern redbud)

Total net benefits	Year 5	Year 10	Year 15	Year 20	Year 25	Year 30	Year 35	Year 40	40-year average
					Dollars				
Yard: west	-16	17	18	19	15	15	14	14	12
Yard: south	-17	15	13	12	7	6	5	5	6
Yard: east	-16	16	16	17	13	12	11	11	10
Public	-23	12	11	10	6	5	4	4	4

Note: Annual values incorporate effects of tree loss. We assume that 10 percent of trees planted die during the first 5 years and 40 percent during the remaining 35 years for a total mortality of 50 percent. See table 6 for annual benefits and table 7 for annual costs.

Table 9—Annual benefits (dollars per tree) at 5-year intervals and 40-year average for a representative medium tree (littleleaf linden)

	Year 5		Year 10		Year 15		Year 20		Year 25		Year 30		Year 35		Year 40		40-year average	
	RU	$	RU	$	RU	$	RU	$	RU	$	RU	$	RU	$	RU	$	RU	$
Cooling (kWh):																		
Yard: west	15	1.02	49	3.36	88	5.98	122	8.30	145	9.89	161	10.93	163	11.10	162	11.05	113	7.70
Yard: south	7	0.47	22	1.50	38	2.58	54	3.69	66	4.48	75	5.09	79	5.38	81	5.52	53	3.59
Yard: east	9	0.60	29	1.97	51	3.46	73	4.96	89	6.02	100	6.78	104	7.04	105	7.14	70	4.75
Public	7	0.47	21	1.41	34	2.34	47	3.23	57	3.85	63	4.31	66	4.49	67	4.55	45	3.08
Heating (therms):																		
Yard: west	0.16	0.16	0.31	0.30	0.31	0.31	0.26	0.25	0.20	0.19	0.19	0.18	0.24	0.23	0.28	0.27	0.24	0.24
Yard: south	0.01	0.01	-0.63	-0.61	-1.80	-1.75	-3.14	-3.05	-4.15	-4.04	-4.76	-4.63	-4.63	-4.63	-4.68	-4.55	-2.99	(2.91)
Yard: east	0.15	0.14	0.22	0.21	0.12	0.12	0.03	0.03	-0.04	-0.04	-0.04	-0.04	0.05	0.04	0.12	0.11	0.08	0.07
Public	0.42	0.41	1.15	1.12	1.83	1.78	2.40	2.33	2.77	2.69	3.03	2.95	3.10	3.02	3.11	3.02	2.23	2.17
Net energy (kWh):																		
Yard: west	166	1.18	524	3.66	911	6.29	1,246	8.55	1,473	10.08	1,626	11.11	1,656	11.33	1,653	11.32	1,157	7.94
Yard: south	71	0.49	158	0.89	199	0.83	228	0.63	244	0.44	273	0.46	315	0.75	344	0.97	229	0.68
Yard: east	102	0.74	311	2.18	522	3.58	732	4.99	882	5.98	993	6.74	1,040	7.09	1,061	7.25	705	4.82
Public	111	0.87	322	2.53	527	4.12	715	5.56	843	6.54	936	7.25	970	7.50	980	7.58	676	5.25
Net carbon dioxide (lb):																		
Yard: west	41	0.14	126	0.42	217	0.73	296	0.99	350	1.17	385	1.29	391	1.30	389	1.30	274	0.92
Yard: south	22	0.07	56	0.19	83	0.28	108	0.36	125	0.42	140	0.47	148	0.50	153	0.51	105	0.35
Yard: east	28	0.09	81	0.27	134	0.45	186	0.62	223	0.75	250	0.83	258	0.86	261	0.87	178	0.59
Public	27	0.09	74	0.25	118	0.40	159	0.53	187	0.62	207	0.69	212	0.71	214	0.71	150	0.50
Air pollution (lb)[a]:																		
Ozone uptake	0.037	0.03	0.112	0.09	0.196	0.16	0.286	0.24	0.366	0.30	0.446	0.37	0.514	0.42	0.581	0.48	0.32	0.26
Nitrogen dioxide uptake+avoided	0.037	0.03	0.116	0.10	0.198	0.16	0.278	0.23	0.336	0.28	0.383	0.32	0.408	0.34	0.425	0.35	0.27	0.22
Sulfur dioxide uptake+avoided	0.118	0.18	0.380	0.57	0.663	0.99	0.933	1.40	1.124	1.69	1.263	1.89	1.314	1.97	1.335	2.00	0.89	1.34
Small particulate matter uptake+avoided	0.013	0.01	0.061	0.06	0.143	0.14	0.253	0.25	0.356	0.35	0.453	0.45	0.457	0.45	0.457	0.45	0.27	0.27
Volatile organic compounds avoided	0.009	0.00	0.030	0.01	0.053	0.02	0.074	0.02	0.089	0.02	0.099	0.03	0.103	0.03	0.104	0.03	0.07	0.02
Biogenic volatile organic compounds released	-0.002	0.00	-0.027	-0.01	-0.079	-0.02	-0.173	-0.05	-0.279	-0.08	-0.378	-0.11	-0.378	-0.11	-0.378	-0.11	-0.21	-0.06
Total air pollution avoided + net uptake	0.212	0.25	0.673	0.82	1.174	1.45	1.650	2.08	1.993	2.56	2.267	2.94	2.416	3.10	2.525	3.20	1.61	2.05
Hydrology (gal)																		
Rainfall interception	203	1.26	630	3.90	1,096	6.80	1,644	10.19	2,136	13.24	2,639	16.36	3,083	19.11	3,526	21.86	1,870	11.59
Aesthetics and other:																		
Yard		9.72		13.19		14.74		14.80		13.88		12.37		10.58		8.71		12.25
Public		10.97		14.87		16.62		16.69		15.65		13.95		11.93		9.82		13.81
Total benefits:																		
Yard: west		12.56		21.99		30.00		36.61		40.93		44.07		45.43		46.39		34.75
Yard: south		11.80		18.99		24.10		28.07		30.54		32.61		34.03		35.26		26.92
Yard: east		12.07		20.36		27.02		32.68		36.41		39.26		40.74		41.90		31.31
Public		13.44		22.37		29.39		35.06		38.62		41.20		42.35		43.18		33.20

Note: Annual values incorporate effects of tree loss. We assume that 10 percent of trees planted die during the first 5 years and 40 percent during the remaining 35 years for a total mortality of 50 percent. RU = resource unit.

[a] Values are the same for yard and public trees.

Table 10—Annual costs (dollars per tree) at 5-year intervals and 40-year average for a representative medium tree (littleleaf linden)

Costs	Year 5	Year 10	Year 15	Year 20	Year 25	Year 30	Year 35	Year 40	40-year average
					Dollars				
Tree and planting[a]:									
Yard	32.00								4.00
Public	31.00								3.88
Pruning:									
Yard	0.29	0.56	4.33	4.20	4.06	3.92	8.83	8.51	3.91
Public	6.56	3.33	5.92	5.60	5.28	4.96	11.12	10.35	6.26
Remove and dispose:									
Yard	0.34	1.39	2.05	2.67	3.25	3.79	4.28	4.73	2.64
Public	0.40	1.26	1.87	2.43	2.96	3.45	3.90	4.31	2.39
Pest and disease									
Yard	0.03	0.06	0.09	0.12	0.14	0.16	0.17	0.18	0.11
Public	0.04	0.08	0.12	0.15	0.17	0.18	0.19	0.20	0.13
Infrastructure repair:									
Yard	0.07	0.13	0.19	0.24	0.28	0.32	0.30	0.37	0.22
Public	0.49	0.94	1.32	1.63	1.87	2.04	2.16	2.22	1.47
Irrigation:									
Yard	0.00	0.00	0.00	0.00	0.00	0.00	0.00	0.00	0.00
Public	1.75	0.00	0.00	0.00	0.00	0.00	0.00	0.00	0.23
Cleanup:									
Yard	0.05	0.09	0.13	0.16	0.19	0.22	0.20	0.25	0.15
Public	0.33	0.65	0.91	1.12	1.29	1.41	1.49	1.53	1.02
Liability and legal:									
Yard	0.00	0.00	0.01	0.01	0.01	0.01	0.01	0.01	0.01
Public	0.02	0.03	0.04	0.05	0.06	0.06	0.07	0.07	0.05
Admin./inspect/other:									
Yard	0.00	0.00	0.00	0.00	0.00	0.00	0.00	0.00	0.00
Public	1.74	3.38	4.74	5.85	6.70	7.33	7.75	7.97	5.30
Total costs:									
Yard	32.77	2.24	6.80	7.40	7.93	8.41	13.79	14.05	10.48
Public	42.33	9.68	14.92	16.82	18.32	19.43	26.67	26.64	18.21

Note: Annual values incorporate effects of tree loss. We assume that 10 percent of trees planted die during the first 5 years and 40 percent during the remaining 35 years for a total mortality of 50 percent. RU = resource unit.

[a] Although tree and planting costs occur in year 1, this value was divided by 5 years to derive an average annual cost for the first 5-year period.

Table 11—Annual net benefits (dollars per tree) at 5-year intervals and 40-year average for a representative medium tree (littleleaf linden)

Total net benefits	Year 5	Year 10	Year 15	Year 20	Year 25	Year 30	Year 35	Year 40	40-year average
					Dollars				
Yard: west	-20	20	23	29	33	36	32	32	24
Yard: south	-21	17	17	21	23	24	20	21	16
Yard: east	-21	18	20	25	28	31	27	28	20
Public	-29	13	14	18	20	22	16	17	12

Note: Annual values incorporate effects of tree loss. We assume that 10 percent of trees planted die during the first 5 years and 40 percent during the remaining 35 years for a total mortality of 50 percent. RU = resource unit. See table 9 for annual benefits and table 10 for annual costs.

Table 12—Annual benefits (dollars per tree) at 5-year intervals and 40-year average for a representative large tree (northern hackberry)

	Year 5		Year 10		Year 15		Year 20		Year 25		Year 30		Year 35		Year 40		40-year average	
	RU	$	RU	$	RU	$	RU	$	RU	$	RU	$	RU	$	RU	$	RU	$
Cooling (kWh):																		
Yard: west	74	5.01	165	11.22	213	14.47	247	16.79	264	17.93	269	18.30	266	18.11	256	17.42	219	14.91
Yard: south	27	1.86	67	4.58	101	6.84	128	8.71	148	10.05	161	10.97	168	11.45	170	11.55	121	8.25
Yard: east	40	2.70	96	6.55	134	9.08	162	11.03	180	12.22	189	12.85	191	13.00	189	12.83	148	10.03
Public	25	1.71	58	3.92	82	5.61	103	7.03	119	8.06	129	8.74	133	9.07	136	9.22	98	6.67
Heating (therms):																		
Yard: west	-0.06	-0.05	-0.27	-0.26	-0.01	-0.01	0.20	0.20	0.37	0.36	0.52	0.51	0.64	0.62	0.70	0.68	0.26	0.26
Yard: south	-2.27	-2.21	-6.49	-6.31	-7.76	-7.55	-8.40	-8.18	-8.31	-8.08	-7.91	-7.69	-7.37	-7.17	-6.73	-6.55	-6.90	-6.72
Yard: east	-0.19	-0.19	-0.55	-0.54	-0.24	-0.23	0.08	0.08	0.39	0.38	0.64	0.62	0.82	0.80	0.93	0.90	0.24	0.23
Public	1.39	1.35	2.82	2.74	3.88	3.78	4.68	4.56	5.15	5.01	5.37	5.22	5.40	5.26	5.25	5.11	4.24	4.13
Net energy (kWh):																		
Yard: west	732	4.96	1,623	10.96	2,127	14.46	2,489	16.99	2,674	18.29	2,744	18.81	2,727	18.73	2,633	18.11	2,219	15.16
Yard: south	46	-0.35	24	-1.73	229	-0.72	440	0.53	646	1.96	823	3.28	947	4.28	1,025	5.00	523	1.53
Yard: east	378	2.51	909	6.02	1,312	8.85	1,631	11.11	1,836	12.60	1,953	13.47	1,994	13.80	1,979	13.73	1,499	10.26
Public	391	3.07	858	6.66	1,213	9.39	1,502	11.58	1,700	13.07	1,823	13.97	1,874	14.33	1,881	14.33	1,405	10.80
Net carbon dioxide (lb):																		
Yard: west	204	0.68	427	1.43	556	1.86	653	2.18	707	2.36	731	2.44	734	2.45	715	2.39	591	1.97
Yard: south	77	0.26	141	0.47	220	0.74	293	0.98	352	1.18	397	1.33	426	1.42	439	1.47	293	0.98
Yard: east	128	0.43	274	0.91	381	1.27	467	1.56	524	1.75	558	1.86	572	1.91	570	1.90	434	1.45
Public	115	0.38	229	0.76	318	1.06	393	1.31	447	1.49	482	1.61	500	1.67	506	1.69	374	1.25
Air pollution (lb)[a]:																		
Ozone uptake	0.125	0.10	0.289	0.24	0.455	0.38	0.620	0.51	0.773	0.64	0.922	0.76	1.059	0.87	1.191	0.98	0.68	0.56
Nitrogen dioxide uptake +avoided	0.146	0.12	0.335	0.28	0.476	0.39	0.594	0.49	0.679	0.56	0.741	0.61	0.780	0.64	0.802	0.66	0.57	0.47
Sulfur dioxide uptake +avoided	0.516	0.77	1.201	1.80	1.656	2.48	2.014	3.02	2.246	3.37	2.384	3.57	2.440	3.66	2.433	3.65	1.86	2.79
Small particulate matter uptake+avoided	0.047	0.05	0.139	0.14	0.254	0.25	0.395	0.39	0.523	0.52	0.641	0.64	0.747	0.74	0.844	0.84	0.45	0.44
Volatile organic compounds avoided	0.041	0.01	0.096	0.03	0.132	0.04	0.160	0.05	0.177	0.05	0.187	0.06	0.190	0.06	0.187	0.06	0.15	0.04
Biogenic volatile organic compounds released	0	0	0	0	0	0	0	0	0	0	0	0	0	0	0	0	0	0
Total air pollution avoided + net uptake	0.876	1.06	2.060	2.48	2.973	3.54	3.783	4.46	4.398	5.14	4.874	5.64	5.215	5.97	5.458	6.19	3.70	4.31
Hydrology (gal)																		
Rainfall interception	959	5.95	2,115	13.11	3,254	20.18	4,390	27.22	5,443	33.75	6,481	40.18	7,439	46.12	8,382	51.97	4,808	29.81
Aesthetics and other:																		
Yard		14.68		22.20		25.89		26.59		25.24		22.61		19.30		15.74		21.53
Public		16.56		25.03		29.19		29.98		28.46		25.50		21.76		17.75		24.28
Total benefits:																		
Yard: west		27.33		50.18		65.92		77.43		84.78		89.69		92.58		94.40		72.79
Yard: south		21.59		36.53		49.63		59.77		67.27		73.04		77.09		80.37		58.16
Yard: east		24.63		44.73		59.73		70.94		78.48		83.77		87.11		89.53		67.36
Public		27.01		48.05		63.36		74.55		81.91		86.90		89.86		91.93		70.45

Note: Annual values incorporate effects of tree loss. We assume that 10 percent of trees planted die during the first 5 years and 40 percent during the remaining 35 years for a total mortality of 50 percent. RU = resource unit.

[a] Values are the same for yard and public trees.

Table 13—Annual costs (dollars per tree) at 5-year intervals and 40-year average for a representative large tree (northern hackberry)

Costs	Year 5	Year 10	Year 15	Year 20	Year 25	Year 30	Year 35	Year 40	40-year average
					Dollars				
Tree and planting[a]:									
Yard	32.00								4.00
Public	31.00								3.88
Pruning:									
Yard	0.29	4.47	4.33	4.20	9.47	9.15	8.83	8.51	5.83
Public	6.56	6.24	5.92	5.60	12.66	11.89	11.12	10.35	8.47
Remove and dispose:									
Yard	1.08	1.51	2.21	2.88	3.52	4.12	4.68	5.22	2.89
Public	2.05	1.37	2.02	2.62	3.20	3.75	4.27	4.75	2.64
Pest and disease									
Yard	0.04	0.07	0.10	0.13	0.15	0.17	0.19	0.20	0.12
Public	0.05	0.09	0.13	0.16	0.18	0.20	0.21	0.22	0.14
Infrastructure repair:									
Yard	0.08	0.14	0.20	0.26	0.30	0.34	0.38	0.40	0.24
Public	0.55	1.02	1.42	1.75	2.02	2.22	2.36	2.45	1.61
Irrigation:									
Yard	0.00	0.00	0.00	0.00	0.00	0.00	0.00	0.00	0.00
Public	1.75	0.00	0.00	0.00	0.00	0.00	0.00	0.00	0.23
Cleanup:									
Yard	0.05	0.10	0.14	0.18	0.21	0.24	0.26	0.28	0.17
Public	0.38	0.71	0.98	1.21	1.39	1.53	1.63	1.69	1.11
Liability and legal:									
Yard	0.00	0.00	0.01	0.01	0.01	0.01	0.01	0.01	0.01
Public	0.02	0.03	0.04	0.06	0.06	0.07	0.07	0.08	0.05
Admin. and other:									
Yard	0.00	0.00	0.00	0.00	0.00	0.00	0.00	0.00	0.00
Public	1.98	3.68	5.12	6.30	7.25	7.97	8.48	8.79	5.78
Total costs:									
Yard	33.54	6.30	7.00	7.65	13.66	14.03	14.35	14.62	13.26
Public	44.34	13.15	15.63	17.71	26.78	27.64	28.15	28.32	23.91

Note: Annual values incorporate effects of tree loss. We assume that 10 percent of trees planted die during the first 5 years and 40 percent during the remaining 35 years for a total mortality of 50 percent.

[a] Although tree and planting costs occur in year 1, this value was divided by 5 years to derive an average annual cost for the first 5-year period.

Table 14—Annual net benefits (dollars per tree) at 5-year intervals and 40-year average for a representative large tree (northern hackberry)

Total net benefits	Year 5	Year 10	Year 15	Year 20	Year 25	Year 30	Year 35	Year 40	40-year average
					Dollars				
Yard: west	-6	44	59	70	71	76	78	80	60
Yard: south	-12	30	43	52	54	59	63	66	45
Yard: east	-9	38	53	63	65	70	73	75	54
Public	-17	35	48	57	55	59	62	64	47

Note: Annual values incorporate effects of tree loss. We assume that 10 percent of trees planted die during the first 5 years and 40 percent during the remaining 35 years for a total mortality of 50 percent.

See table 12 for annual benefits and table 13 for annual costs.

Appendix 3: Procedures for Estimating Benefits and Costs

Approach

Pricing Benefits and Costs

In this study, annual benefits and costs over a 40-year planning horizon were estimated for newly planted trees in three residential yard locations (east, south, and west of the dwelling unit) and a public streetside or park location. Trees in these hypothetical locations are called "yard" and "public" trees, respectively. Prices were assigned to each cost (e.g., planting, pruning, removal, irrigation, infrastructure repair, liability) and benefit (e.g., heating/cooling, energy savings, air-pollution reduction, stormwater-runoff reduction) through direct estimation and implied valuation of benefits as environmental externalities. This approach made it possible to estimate the net benefits of plantings in "typical" locations with "typical" tree species.

To account for differences in the mature size and growth rates of different tree species, we report results for a small (eastern redbud), medium (littleleaf linden), and large (northern hackberry) deciduous tree (see "Common and Scientific Names" section). Results are reported for 5-year intervals for 40 years.

Mature tree height is frequently used to characterize small, medium, and large species because matching tree height to available overhead space is an important design consideration. However, in this analysis, leaf surface area (LSA) and crown diameter were also used to characterize **mature tree size**. These additional measurements are useful indicators for many functional benefits of trees that relate to leaf-atmosphere processes (e.g., interception, transpiration, **photosynthesis**). Tree growth rates, dimensions, and LSA estimates are based on tree growth modeling.

Growth Modeling

Growth models are based on data collected in Indianapolis, Indiana. The city's Parks and Recreation Department Forestry Section provided an inventory of Indianapolis's municipal trees that included 117,525 trees.

Tree-growth models developed from Indianapolis data were used as the basis for modeling tree growth for this report. Using Indianapolis's tree inventory, we measured a stratified random sample of 19 of the most common tree species to establish relations between tree age, size, leaf area, and biomass. The species were as follows:

- Norway maple (*Acer platanoides* L.)
- Red maple (*Acer rubrum* L.)
- Silver maple (*Acer saccharinum* L.)
- Sugar maple (*Acer saccharum* Michx.)
- Northern catalpa (*Catalpa speciosa* (Warder) Warder ex Engelm.)
- Eastern redbud (*Cercis canadensis* L.)
- Northern hackberry (*Celtis occidentalis* L.)
- White ash (*Fraxinus americana* L.)
- Green ash (*Fraxinus pennsylvanica* Marsh.)
- Honeylocust (*Gleditsia triacanthos* L.)
- Black walnut (*Juglans nigra* L.)
- Crabapple (*Malus* spp.)
- Mulberry (*Morus* spp.)
- Blue spruce (*Picea pungens* Engelm.)
- Eastern white pine (*Pinus strobus* L.)
- Eastern cottonwood (*Populus deltoids* Bartram ex Marsh.)
- Callery pear (*Pyrus calleryana* Dcne.)
- Northern red oak (*Quercus rubra* L.)
- Littleleaf linden (*Tilia cordata* Mill.)
- Siberian elm (*Ulmus pumila* L.)

For the growth models, information spanning the life cycle of predominant tree species was collected. The inventory was stratified into the following nine diameter-at-breast-height (d.b.h.) classes:

- 0 to 2.9 in
- 3.0 to 5.9 in
- 6.0 to 11.9 in
- 12.0 to 17.9 in
- 18.0 to 23.9 in
- 24.0 to 29.9 in
- 30.0 to 35.9 in
- 36.0 to 41.9 in
- >42.0 in

Thirty to sixty trees of each species were randomly selected for surveying, along with an equal number of alternative trees. Tree measurements included d.b.h. (to nearest 0.1 cm [0.04 in] by sonar measuring device), tree crown height, and bole height (to nearest 0.5 m [1.6 ft] by clinometer), crown diameter in two directions (parallel and perpendicular to nearest street to nearest 0.5 m [1.6 ft] by sonar measuring device), tree condition, and location. Replacement trees were sampled when trees from the original sample population could not be located. Tree age was determined by street-tree managers. Field work was conducted in August 2006.

Crown volume and leaf area were estimated from computer processing of tree-crown images obtained with a digital camera. The method has shown greater accuracy than other techniques (±20 percent of actual leaf area) in estimating crown volume and leaf area of open-grown trees (Peper and McPherson 2003).

Linear and logarithmic regression was used to fit predictive models with d.b.h. as a function of age for each of the 20 sampled species. Predictions of LSA, crown diameter, and height metrics were modeled as a function of d.b.h. by using best-fit models. After inspecting the growth curves for each species, we selected the typical small, medium, and large tree species for this report.

Reporting Results

Results are reported in terms of annual values per tree planted. However, to make these calculations realistic, mortality rates are included. Based on our survey of regional municipal foresters and commercial arborists, this analysis assumed that 50 percent of the hypothetical planted trees died over the 40-year period. Annual mortality rates were 2.0 percent for the first 5 years, and 1.14 percent per year after that. The accounting approach "grows" trees in different locations and uses computer simulation to directly calculate the annual flow of benefits and costs as trees mature and die (McPherson 1992).

Benefits and costs are directly connected with tree-size variables such as trunk d.b.h., tree canopy cover, and LSA. For instance, pruning and removal costs usually increase with tree size, expressed as d.b.h. For some parameters, such as sidewalk repair, costs are negligible for young trees but increase relatively rapidly as tree roots grow large enough to heave pavement. For other parameters, such as air-pollutant uptake and rainfall interception, benefits are related to tree canopy cover and leaf area.

Most benefits occur on an annual basis, but some costs are periodic. For instance, street trees may be pruned on regular cycles but are removed in a less regular fashion (e.g., when they pose a hazard or soon after they die). In this analysis, most costs and benefits are reported for the year in which they occur.

However, periodic costs such as pruning, pest and disease control, and infrastructure repair are presented on an average annual basis. Although spreading one-time costs over each year of a maintenance cycle does not alter the 40-year nominal expenditure, it can lead to inaccuracies if future costs are discounted to the present.

Benefit and Cost Valuation

Source of cost estimates

Frequency and costs of tree management were estimated based on surveys with municipal foresters from Indianapolis, Carmel, and Terre Haute, Indiana, and Marietta and Cincinnati, Ohio. Several arborists from Brownsburg, Carmel, and Indianapolis, Indiana, and Columbus and Gallipolos, Ohio, provided information on tree management costs on residential properties.

Monetizing benefits

To monetize effects of trees on energy use, we take the perspective of a residential customer by using retail electricity and natural-gas prices for utilities serving the Lower Midwest, including Indianapolis and Louisville, Kentucky. The retail price of energy reflects a full accounting of costs as paid by the end user, such as the utility costs of power generation, transmission, distribution, administration, marketing, and profit. This perspective aligns with our modeling method, which calculates energy effects of trees based on differences among consumers in heating and air conditioning equipment types, saturations, building construction types, and base loads.

The preferred way to value air quality benefits from trees is to first determine the costs of damages to human health from polluted air, then calculate the value of avoided costs because trees are cleaning the air. Economic valuation of damages to human health usually uses information on willingness to pay to avoid damages obtained via interviews or direct estimates of the monetary costs of damages (e.g., alleviating headaches, extending life). Empirical correlations developed by Wang and Santini (1995) reviewed 5 studies and 15 sets of regional cost data to relate per-ton costs of various pollutant emissions to regional ambient air quality measurements and population size. We use their damage-based estimates unless the values are negative, in which case we use their control-cost-based estimates.

Calculating Benefits

Calculating Energy Benefits

The prototypical building used as a basis for the simulations was typical of post-1980 construction practices and represents approximately one-third of the total single-family residential housing stock in the Lower Midwest region. The house was a one-story, wood-frame, slab-on-grade building with a conditioned floor area of 2,070 ft², window area (double-glazed) of 263 ft², and wall and ceiling insulation of R13 and R31, respectively. The central cooling system had a **seasonal energy efficiency ratio (SEER)** of 10, and the natural-gas furnace had an **annual fuel utilization efficiency (AFUE)** of 78 percent. Building footprints were square, reflecting average impacts for a large number of buildings (McPherson and Simpson 1999). Buildings were simulated with 1.5-ft overhangs. Blinds had a visual density of 37 percent and were assumed to be closed when the air conditioner was operating. Summer thermostat settings were 78 °F; winter settings were 68 °F during the day and 60 °F at night. Because the prototype building was larger, but more energy efficient, than most other construction types, our projected energy savings can be considered similar to those for older, less thermally efficient, but smaller buildings. The energy simulations relied on typical meteorological data from Indianapolis (Marion and Urban 1995).

Calculating energy savings

The dollar value of energy savings was based on regional average residential electricity and natural-gas prices of $0.068/**kWh** and $0.973/**therm** (Indianapolis Power and Light Company 2007, Citizens Gas and Coke Utility 2007). Homes were assumed to have central air conditioning and natural-gas heating.

Calculating shade effects

Residential yard trees were within 60 ft of homes so as to directly shade walls and windows. **Shade effects** of these trees on building energy use were simulated for small, medium, and large trees at three tree-to-building distances, following methods outlined by McPherson and Simpson (1999). Results of shade effects for each tree were averaged over distance and weighted by occurrence within each of three distance classes: 28 percent at 10 to 20 ft (3 to 6 m), 68 percent at 20 to 40 ft (6 to 12 m), and 4 percent at 40 to 60 ft (12 to 18 m) (McPherson and Simpson 1999).

The small tree (eastern redbud) had visual densities of 70 percent during summer and 25 percent during winter, the medium tree (littleleaf linden) had visual densities of 59 percent during summer and 12 percent during winter, and the large tree (northern hackberry) had visual densities of 53 percent during summer and 12 percent during winter.

Leaf-off values for use in calculating winter shade were based on published values where available (Hammond et al. 1980, McPherson 1984). Foliation periods for deciduous trees were obtained from the literature (Hammond et al. 1980, McPherson 1984) and adjusted for Indianapolis based on consultation with the city arborist (Pinco 2007). The foliation periods of the small, medium, and larger trees were 24 April–31 October.

Results are reported for trees shading east-, south-, and west-facing surfaces. Our results for public trees are conservative in that we assumed that they do not provide shading benefits. For example, in Modesto, California, 15 percent of total annual dollar energy savings from street trees was due to shade and 85 percent due to **climate effects** (McPherson et al. 1999a).

Calculating climate effects

In addition to localized shade effects, which were assumed to accrue only to residential yard trees, lowered air temperatures and windspeeds from increased neighborhood tree cover (referred to as climate effects) produced a net decrease in demand for winter heating and summer cooling (reduced windspeeds by themselves may increase or decrease cooling demand, depending on the circumstances). Climate effects on energy use, air temperature, and windspeed, as a function of neighborhood canopy cover, were estimated from published values (McPherson and Simpson 1999). Existing tree canopy plus building cover was 26 percent based on estimates of urban tree cover for Indiana (Nowak and Crane 2002). Canopy cover was calculated to increase by 3.1 percent, 4.6 percent, and 10.1 percent for 20-year-old small, medium, and large deciduous and coniferous trees, respectively, based on an effective lot size (actual lot size plus a portion of adjacent street and other rights-of-way) of 10,000 ft^2, and one tree on average was assumed per lot. Climate effects were estimated by simulating effects of wind reductions and air-temperature reductions on energy use. Climate effects accrued for both public and yard trees.

Atmospheric Carbon Dioxide Reduction

Calculating reduction in CO_2 emissions from powerplants

Conserving energy in buildings can reduce carbon dioxide (CO_2) emissions from powerplants. Emission reductions were calculated as the product of energy savings for heating and cooling with CO_2 **emission factors** (table 15) based on data for Indianapolis Power and Light Company, the local utility company in Indianapolis, where the average fuel mix consists almost entirely of fossil fuels (99.9 percent) power (U.S. EPA 2006). The value of $6.68 per ton CO_2 reduction (table 15) was based on the average value given by Pearce (2003).

Calculating carbon storage

Sequestration, the net rate of CO_2 storage in above- and belowground biomass over the course of one growing season, was calculated from tree height and d.b.h. data with volume equations (McHale et al., in press; Pillsbury et al. 1998). Volume estimates were converted to green- and dry-weight estimates (Alden 1995, Markwardt 1930) and divided by 78 percent to incorporate root biomass. Dry-weight biomass was converted to carbon (50 percent) and these values were converted to CO_2. The amount of CO_2 sequestered each year is the annual increment of CO_2 stored as trees increase their biomass. There were four species for which no urban tree volume equations were available. Harris' general hardwoods biomass equation was used to estimate biomass for pear, crabapple, and American holly (Tritton and Hornbeck 1982). Red maple biomass was estimated using a forest-derived biomass equation (Ter-Mikaelian and Korzukhin 1997) with resulting estimates reduced by 20 percent to reflect the lower woody biomass levels of open-grown trees.

Table 15—Emissions factors and implied values for carbon dioxide and criteria air pollutants

Emission factor	Electricity[a]	Natural gas[b]	Implied value[c]
	Pounds per megawatt hour	*Pounds per therm*	*Dollars per pound*
Carbon dioxide	2,180	11.8	0.00334
Nitrogen dioxide	2.968	0.01020	0.82
Sulfur dioxide	11.966	0.00006	1.50
Small particulate matter	1.000	0.00075	0.99
Volatile organic compounds	0.999	0.00054	0.30

[a] U.S. EPA 2003, except Ottinger et al. 1990 for volatile organic compounds.

[b] U.S. EPA 1998.

[c] Carbon dioxide from Pearce 2003. Value for others based on methods of Wang and Santini (1995) using emissions concentrations from U.S. EPA (2003) and population estimates from the U.S. Census Bureau (2006).

Calculating CO_2 released by power equipment

Tree-related CO_2 emissions, based on gasoline and diesel fuel consumption during tree care in our survey cities, were calculated by using the value 0.502 lbs of CO_2 per in d.b.h. (Pinco 2007). This amount may overestimate CO_2 release associated with less intensively maintained residential yard trees.

Calculating CO_2 released during decomposition

To calculate CO_2 released through decomposition of dead woody biomass, we conservatively estimated that dead trees were removed and mulched in the year that death occurred, and that 80 percent of their stored carbon was released to the atmosphere as CO_2 in the same year (McPherson and Simpson 1999).

Calculating Reduction in Air Pollutant Emissions

Reductions in building energy use also result in reduced emission of air pollutants from powerplants and space-heating equipment. Volatile organic hydrocarbons (VOCs) and nitrogen dioxide (NO_2)—both precursors of ozone (O_3) formation—as well as sulfur dioxide (SO_2) and particulate matter <10 microns in diameter (PM_{10}) were considered. Changes in average annual emissions and their monetary values were calculated in the same way as for CO_2, with utility-specific emissions factors for electricity and heating fuels (Ottinger et al. 1990, U.S. EPA 1998). The price of emissions savings was derived from models that calculate the marginal cost of controlling different pollutants to meet air quality standards (Wang and Santini 1995). Emissions concentrations were obtained from U.S. EPA (2003) (table 15), and population estimates from the U.S. Census Bureau (2006).

Calculating pollutant uptake by trees

Trees also remove pollutants from the atmosphere. The modeling method we applied was developed by Scott et al. (1998). It calculates **hourly pollutant dry deposition** per tree expressed as the product of deposition velocity ($V_d = 1/[R_a + R_b + R_c]$), pollutant concentration (C), canopy-projection area (CP), and a time step, where R_a, R_b, and R_c are aerodynamic, boundary layer, and stomatal resistances. Hourly deposition velocities for each pollutant were calculated during the growing season by using estimates for the resistances ($R_a + R_b + R_c$) for each hour throughout the year. Hourly concentrations for O_3, PM_{10}, SO_2, and NO_2 for Indianapolis,

Indiana, were obtained from the Environmental Protection Agency (U.S. EPA 2007), as well as hourly meteorological data (i.e., air temperature, windspeed, solar radiation. The year 2003 was chosen because it most closely approximated long-term, regional climate records. To set a value for pollutant uptake by trees, we used the procedure described above for emissions reductions (table 15). The monetary value for NO_2 was used for ozone.

Estimating BVOC emissions from trees

Annual emissions for biogenic volatile organic compounds (BVOCs) were esti-mated for the four tree species by using the algorithms of Guenther et al. (1991, 1993). Annual emissions were simulated during the growing season over 40 years. The emission of carbon as isoprene was expressed as a product of the base emission rate (μg C per g dry foliar biomass per h), adjusted for sunlight and temperature and the amount of dry, foliar biomass present in the tree. Monoterpene emissions were estimated by using a base emission rate adjusted for temperature. The base emission rates for the four species were based on values reported in the literature (Benjamin and Winer 1998). Hourly emissions were summed to get monthly and annual emissions.

Annual dry foliar biomass was derived from field data collected in Indianapo-lis, Indiana, during August 2006. The amount of foliar biomass present for each year of the simulated tree's life was unique for each species. Hourly air tempera-ture and solar radiation data for 2003 described in the pollutant uptake section were used as model inputs.

Calculating net air quality benefits

Net air quality benefits were calculated by subtracting the costs associated with BVOC emissions from benefits associated with pollutant uptake and avoided power-plant emissions. The O_3-reduction benefit from lowering summertime air tempera-tures, thereby reducing hydrocarbon emissions from **anthropogenic** and **biogenic** sources, was estimated as a function of canopy cover following McPherson and Simpson (1999). Hourly changes in air temperature were calculated by reducing this peak air temperature at every hour based on hourly maximum and minimum temperature for that day, scaled by magnitude of maximum total global solar radiation for each day relative to the maximum value for the year.

Stormwater Benefits

Estimating rainfall interception by tree canopies

A numerical simulation model was used to estimate annual rainfall interception (Xiao et al. 2000). The interception model accounted for water intercepted by the tree, as well as **throughfall** and **stem flow**. Intercepted water is stored temporarily on canopy leaf and bark surfaces. Rainwater evaporates or drips from leaf surfaces and flows down the stem surface to the ground. Tree-canopy parameters that affect interception include species, leaf and stem surface areas, **shade coefficients** (visual density of the crown), foliation periods, and tree dimensions (e.g., tree height, crown height, crown diameter, and d.b.h.). Tree-height data were used to estimate windspeed at different heights above the ground and resulting rates of evaporation.

The volume of water stored in the tree crown was calculated from crown-projection area (area under tree **dripline**), **leaf area indices** (LAI, the ratio of LSA to crown projection area), and the depth of water captured by the canopy surface. Gap fractions, foliation periods, and **tree surface saturation storage capacity** influence the amount of projected throughfall. Tree surface saturation was 1.0 mm (0.04 in) for all trees.

Hourly meteorological and rainfall data for 2005 at the Indianapolis International Airport (IND) (Latitude: 39.717°, Longitude: -86.267°, Elevation: 790 ft, NOAA COOPID: 124259) in Indianapolis, Indiana, were used in this simulation. The year 2005 was chosen because, although the overall amount of rainfall was higher, it most closely approximated the monthly distribution of the long-term average rainfall. Annual precipitation at IND during 2005 was 43.7 in, which is slightly higher than long-time annual average precipitation (42.5 in). Storm events less than 0.1 in were assumed not to produce runoff and were dropped from the analysis. More complete descriptions of the interception model can be found in Xiao et al. (1998, 2000).

Calculating water quality protection and flood control benefit

The benefits that result from reduced peak runoff include reduced property damage from flooding and reduced loss of soil and habitat from erosion and sediment flow. Reduced runoff also results in improved water quality in streams, lakes, and rivers. This can translate into improved aquatic habitats, less human illness owing to reduced contact with contaminated water and reduced stormwater treatment costs.

According to Brian Brown, the city of Indianapolis spends approximately $21 million annually on operations and maintenance of its stormwater management system (Brown 2007). In addition, the Clean Streams-Healthy Neighborhoods program is an investment of more than $3 billion over 20 years (Ray 2007). Thus, total annual expenditures including capital improvements are $171 million. To calculate annual runoff, we assigned curve numbers for each land use (USDA SCS 1986). Land use percentages were obtained from the city land use GIS layers (Purcell 2007). We calculated runoff depth for each land use (5.7 in citywide) and found the citywide total to be 84,956 acre-feet. The annual stormwater control cost was estimated to be $0.006 per gallon of runoff.

Aesthetic and Other Benefits

Many benefits attributed to urban trees are difficult to translate into economic terms. Beautification, privacy, wildlife habitat, shade that increases human comfort, sense of place and well-being are services that are difficult to price. However, the value of some of these benefits may be captured in the property values of the land on which trees stand.

To estimate the value of these "other" benefits, we applied results of research that compared differences in sales prices of houses to statistically quantify the difference associated with trees. All else being equal, the difference in sales price reflects the willingness of buyers to pay for the benefits and costs associated with trees. This approach has the virtue of capturing in the sales price both the benefits and costs of trees as perceived by the buyers. Limitations to this approach include difficulty determining the value of individual trees on a property, the need to extrapolate results from studies done years ago, and the need to extrapolate results from front-yard trees on residential properties to trees in other locations (e.g., back yards, streets, parks, and nonresidential land).

Anderson and Cordell (1988) surveyed 844 single-family residences in Athens, Georgia, and found that each large front-yard tree was associated with a 0.88-percent increase in the average home sales price. This percentage of sales price was used as an indicator of the additional value a resident in the Lower Midwest region would gain from selling a home with a large tree.

We used the average median home price for Indianapolis, Indiana, St. Louis, Missouri, Lexington and Louisville, Kentucky, Cincinnati and Dayton, Ohio ($135,400), as our starting point. Therefore, the value of a large tree that added 0.88 percent to the sales price of such a home was $1,192. To estimate annual benefits, the total added value was divided by the LSA of a 30-year-old green ash ($1,192 per 4,076 ft^2) to yield the base value of LSA, $0.292 per ft^2. This value was multiplied by the amount of LSA added to the tree during 1 year of growth.

Additionally, not all street trees are as effective as front-yard trees in increasing property values. For example, trees adjacent to multifamily housing units will not increase the property value at the same rate as trees in front of single-family homes. Therefore, a citywide street tree reduction factor (0.83) was applied to prorate trees' value based on the assumption that trees adjacent to different land uses make different contributions to property sales prices. For this analysis, the street reduction factor reflects the distribution of street trees in Indianapolis by land use. Reduction factors were single-home residential (100 percent), multihome residential (75 percent), small commercial (66 percent), industrial/institutional/ large commercial (66 percent), park/vacant/other (50 percent) (Gonzales 2004, McPherson 2001).

Calculating the aesthetic and other benefits of residential yard trees

To calculate the base value for a large tree on private residential property we assumed that a 30-year-old white ash in the front yard increased the property sales price by $1,192. Approximately 75 percent of all yard trees, however, are in back yards (Richards et al. 1984). Lacking specific research findings, it was assumed that back-yard trees had 75 percent of the impact on "curb appeal" and sales price compared to front-yard trees. The average annual aesthetic and other benefits for a tree on private property were, therefore, estimated as $0.21 per ft^2 LSA. To estimate annual benefits, this value was multiplied by the amount of LSA added to the tree during 1 year of growth.

Calculating the aesthetic value of a public tree

The base value of street trees was calculated in the same way as yard trees. However, because street trees may be adjacent to land with little resale potential, an adjusted value was calculated. An analysis of street trees in Modesto, California, sampled from aerial photographs (sample size 8 percent of street trees), found that 15 percent were located adjacent to nonresidential or commercial property (McPherson et al. 1999a). We assumed that 33 percent of these trees—or 5 percent of the entire street-tree population—produced no benefits associated with property value increases.

Although the impact of parks on real estate values has been reported (Hammer et al. 1974, Schroeder 1982, Tyrvainen 1999), to our knowledge, the onsite and external benefits of park trees alone have not been isolated (More et al. 1988).

After reviewing the literature and recognizing an absence of data, we made the conservative estimate that park trees had half the impact on property prices of street trees.

Given these assumptions, typical large street and park trees were estimated to increase property values by $0.27 and $0.15 per ft^2 LSA, respectively. Assuming that 80 percent of all municipal trees were on streets and 20 percent in parks, a weighted average benefit of $0.251/$ft^2$ LSA was calculated for each tree.

Calculating Costs

Tree management costs were estimated based on surveys with municipal foresters from Carmel, Indianapolis, and Terre Haute, Indiana, and Cincinnati and Marietta, Ohio. In addition, several commercial arborists from Brownsburg, Carmel, and Indianapolis, Indiana, and Gallipolos and Columbus, Ohio, provided information on tree management costs on residential properties.

Planting

Planting costs include the cost of the tree and the cost for planting, staking, and mulching the tree. Based on our survey of Lower Midwest municipal and commercial arborists, planting costs ranged widely from $106 for a 2-in d.b.h. tree to $550 for a 5-in tree. In this analysis we assumed that a 2-in yard tree was planted at a cost of $160. The cost for planting a 2-in public tree was $155.

Pruning
Pruning costs for public trees

After studying data from municipal forestry programs and their contractors, we assumed that young public trees were inspected and pruned once every 2 years during the first 5 years after planting at a cost of $15 per tree. After this training period, inspection and pruning occurred once every 5 years for small trees (< 20 ft tall) at $20 per tree. More expensive equipment and more time was required to prune medium trees once every 8 years ($60 per tree) and large trees once every 10 years ($180 per tree). After factoring in pruning frequency, annualized costs were $7.50, $4, $7.50, and $18 per tree for public young, small, medium, and large trees, respectively.

Pruning costs for yard trees

Based on findings from our survey of commercial arborists in the Lower Midwest region, pruning cycles for yard trees were 2, 3, 5, and 7 years for young, small, medium, and large trees, respectively. Only about 20 percent of all private trees were professionally pruned (**contract rate**), although the number of professionally pruned trees grows as the trees grow. We assumed that professionals are paid to prune all large trees, 60 percent of the medium trees, and only 6 percent of the small and young trees and conifers (Summit and McPherson 1998). Using these contract rates, along with average pruning prices ($50, $100, $200, and $400 for young, small, medium, and large trees, respectively), the average annual costs for pruning a yard tree were $0.30, $0.60, $4.80, and $11.20 for young, small, medium, and large trees, respectively.

Tree and Stump Removal

The costs for tree removal and disposal were $20 per in d.b.h. for public trees, and $35 per in d.b.h. for yard trees. Stump removal costs were $6 per in d.b.h. for public trees and $7 per in d.b.h. for yard trees. Therefore, total costs for removal and disposal of trees and stumps were $26 per in d.b.h. for public trees, and $42 per in d.b.h. for yard trees. Removal costs of trees less than 3 inches in diameter were $16 for public trees and $80 for yard trees.

Irrigation Costs

Costs for watering during the critical 5-year establishment period were estimated at $2.00 for public trees per tree per year, mainly for the labor costs involved in visiting the trees with a water truck or other time-intensive method. Beyond the establishment period, it is assumed that trees have been planted into irrigated landscapes and therefore the cost of additional water for the trees is negligible. No costs for irrigating yard trees were included because these were also assumed to be planted in irrigated landscapes where the cost of additional water is negligible and the additional labor involved for extra watering during the first 5 years by the resident was also considered negligible.

Pest and Disease Control

Pest and disease control measures in the Lower Midwest are minimal, with cities spending only about $0.16 per tree per year and residential arborists $0.11 per tree per year.

Other Costs for Public and Yard Trees

Other costs associated with the management of trees include expenditures for infrastructure repair/root pruning, leaf-litter cleanup, and inspection/administration.

Infrastructure conflict costs

As trees and sidewalks age, roots can cause damage to sidewalks, curbs, paving, and sewer lines. Sidewalk repair is typically one of the largest expenses for public trees (McPherson and Peper 1995). Infrastructure-related expenditures for public trees in Lower Midwest communities were approximately $2.23 per tree on an annual basis. Roots from most trees in yards do not damage sidewalks and sewers. Therefore, the cost for yard trees was estimated to be only 10 percent of the cost for public trees.

Litter and storm cleanup costs

The average annual cost per tree for litter cleanup (i.e., street sweeping, storm-damage cleanup) was $1.54 per tree ($0.135 per in d.b.h.). This value was based on average annual litter cleanup costs and storm cleanup, assuming a large storm results in extraordinary costs about once a decade. Because most residential yard trees are not littering the streets with leaves, it was assumed that cleanup costs for yard trees were 10 percent of those for public trees.

Inspection and administration costs

Municipal tree programs have administrative costs for salaries of supervisors and clerical staff, operating costs, and overhead. Our survey found that the average annual cost for inspection and administration associated with street- and park-tree management was $6.41 per tree ($0.703 per in d.b.h.). Trees on private property do not accrue this expense.

Calculating Net Benefits

Benefits Accrue at Different Scales

When calculating net benefits, it is important to recognize that trees produce benefits that accrue both on- and offsite. Benefits are realized at four scales: parcel, neighborhood, community, and global. For example, property owners with onsite trees not only benefit from increased property values, but they may also directly benefit from improved human health (e.g., reduced exposure to cancer-causing ultraviolet radiation) and greater psychological well-being through visual and direct contact with plants. However, on the cost side, increased health care costs owing to allergies and respiratory ailments related to pollen may be incurred because of nearby trees. We assume that these intangible benefits and costs are reflected in what we term "aesthetics and other benefits."

The property owner can obtain additional economic benefits from onsite trees depending on their location and condition. For example, carefully located onsite trees can provide air-conditioning savings by shading windows and walls and cooling building microclimates. This benefit can extend to adjacent neighbors who benefit from shade and air-temperature reductions that lower their cooling costs.

Neighborhood attractiveness and property values can be influenced by the extent of tree canopy cover on individual properties. At the community scale, benefits are realized through cleaner air and water, as well as social, educational, and employment and job training benefits that can reduce costs for health care, welfare, crime prevention, and other social service programs.

Reductions in atmospheric CO_2 concentrations owing to trees are an example of benefits that are realized at the global scale.

Annual benefits are calculated as:

$$B = E + AQ + CO_2 + H + A$$

where

E = value of net annual energy savings (cooling and heating)

AQ = value of annual air-quality improvement (pollutant uptake, avoided powerplant emissions, and BVOC emissions)

CO_2 = value of annual CO_2 reductions (sequestration, avoided emissions, release from tree care and decomposition)

H = value of annual stormwater-runoff reductions

A = value of annual aesthetics and other benefits

On the other side of the benefit-cost equation are costs for tree planting and management. Expenditures are borne by property owners (irrigation, pruning, and removal) and the community (pollen and other health care costs). Annual costs (C) are the sum of costs for residential yard trees (C_Y) and public trees (C_P) where:

$$C_Y = P + T + R + D + I + S + Cl + L$$
$$C_P = P + T + R + D + I + S + Cl + L + A \text{ where}$$

P = cost of tree and planting

T = average annual tree pruning cost

R = annualized tree and stump removal and disposal cost

D = average annual pest- and disease-control cost

I = annual irrigation cost

S = average annual cost to repair/mitigate infrastructure damage

Cl = annual litter and storm cleanup cost

L = average annual cost for litigation and settlements from tree-related claims

A = annual program administration, inspection, and other costs

Net benefits are calculated as the difference between total benefits and costs:

Net benefits = $B - C$

Benefit-cost ratios (BCR) are calculated as the ratio of benefits to costs:

BCR = B / C

Limitations of This Study

This analysis does not account for the wide variety of trees planted in Lower Midwest communities or their diverse placement. It does not incorporate the full range of climatic differences within the region that influence potential energy, air-quality, and hydrology benefits. Estimating aesthetics and other benefits is difficult because the research in this area is not well developed. We considered only residential and municipal tree cost scenarios, but realize that the costs associated with planting and managing trees can differ widely depending on program characteristics. For example, our analysis does not incorporate costs incurred by utility companies and passed on to customers for maintenance of trees under power lines. However, as described by examples in chapter 3, local cost data can be substituted for the data in this report to evaluate the benefits and costs of alternative programs.

In this analysis, results are presented in terms of future values of benefits and costs, not present values. Thus, findings do not incorporate the time value of money or inflation. We assume that the user intends to invest in community forests and our objective is to identify the relative magnitudes of future costs and benefits. If the user is interested in comparing an investment in urban forestry with other investment opportunities, it is important to discount all future benefits and costs to the beginning of the investment period. For example, trees with a future value of $100,000 in 10 years have a present value of $55,840, assuming a 6-percent annual interest rate.

This publication is available online at www.fs.fed.us/psw/. You may also order additional copies of it by sending your mailing information in label form through one of the following means. Please specify the publication title and series number.

Fort Collins Service Center

Web site	http://www.fs.fed.us/psw/
Telephone	(970) 498 1392
FAX	(970) 498 1122
E-mail	rschneider@fs.fed.us
Mailing address	Publications Distribution
	Rocky Mountain Research Station
	240 West Prospect Road
	Fort Collins, CO 80526 2098

Pacific Southwest Research Station
800 Buchanan Street
Albany, CA 94710

Federal Recycling Program
Printed on Recycled Paper